MW00532419

PETER CAUGHEY

LIVING
WITH A FULL CUP
BE PRESENT, BE HAPPY, SEE THE BIG PICTURE

This book is for all the students and patients who have attended my classes and come to my clinic throughout the years - and for my friends. Thank you for sharing with me the seeking of truth and meaning in our lives.

ACKNOWLEDGEMENTS

The development of this book has truly been a team effort. I would firstly like to thank my students, my patients and my friends for their support over the years. I owe this book to them for their encouragement to document my stories, my thoughts and my experiences in my life and write them down and to share them with other people.

A big thank you to my friend Phil Doyle, not only for inspiring me, but for his guidance in the structure in the early manuscripts for this book.

My deepest gratitude to Amanda Kimmerly for the final editing and shaping of this book. Thank you for all your time and expert guidance.

To Nita for the time spent deciphering my handwritten pieces of paper and making some sense of my arrows, cross-outs, hard to read handwriting and creative spelling.

And so importantly, to my dearest Josephine. It is difficult to put into words my thanks to her for her tirelessly reading and editing of my writing. Her help with formatting and structuring this book. And most importantly, for all her support in bringing these words to print to share with people and the world. You are my best friend and love of my life.

INTRODUCTION

For most of my life, I have had these burning questions: Why am I here? Why was I born onto this planet? What is my real purpose?

I started my journey of discovery early in life and like many people, I started reading spiritual books and investigating religious teachings from many spiritual modalities. I knew there had to be more to my existence than having a job, buying a house, getting married, and having children. More than a three-week holiday once a year, growing old, and dying.

In my life's voyage, I have discovered that there is something wildly profound running in the background: an invisible force that didn't really become apparent until I met my first spiritual teacher. I always seem to find the right person at the right time to help me find the answers to my questions, and no one has been more pertinent and timely than my first Taiji Master who, at a time of great grief, opened me up to a new way of life and helped me see the world through different eyes. Using the philosophy of the Taiji Monastery School, he taught me how to see and understand myself and to appreciate and value my involvement with other people, the world, and life in a completely new way.

In this book, I share part of my journey, the venture into the truth behind my beliefs, opinions, and points of view. It is my journey into uncovering the stories of what I believed in my life and what I thought the world was all about. I discovered the way I saw the world (and what I thought we should or shouldn't do and how we should or shouldn't behave) wasn't necessarily true. What I was taught by parents, teachers, friends, family, and my community - and by society as a whole - were just human-made beliefs, opinions, and a constructed way of how to live. I questioned and challenged these points of views and this way of seeing and living in the world. It led me to believe there is another way.

I observed myself reacting to the way I was told to live, behave, and think. I observed disparities in the words and the actions of others. I watched people defending their beliefs and opinions as if they were the "Truth," becoming the basis for constant wars, conflicts, and disagreements with each other. But are these beliefs and stories that we defend with our lives really true, or are they just opinions?

To discover who we really are and to be truly free, we need to uncover what stories are running in the background driving us. Then we need to challenge these core beliefs and opinions. Question their origins. Where did they really come from, and who told us they were true? To be truly free, we have to see beyond any stories we have of how the world should be and how we should live our lives.

In this book, I will share with you my journey into the origins and the validity of these beliefs and unconscious ways to see life. I discuss how I identified some of these stories, how they were affecting my life, how I broke free from them, as well as the flow on effect of not having them drive my life anymore.

I initially started sharing my experiences and life-changing events through blog posts. I received so much positive feedback and response that I realized others had the same stories and beliefs as

I did. I decided the best way to help others make some sense out of their own dilemmas was to refine the insights I had gained and to put them in a book. I believe this is a perfect time to release this book as more and more people, patients, and students are asking me the same questions. They all seem to be looking for the same answers to "What is the purpose to life?"

Hopefully this book will bring clarity to this question. I'm certainly not saying I have all the answers, but maybe I can share some understanding on the unconscious stories I have discovered that are driving most people, and if nothing else, it will be food for thought.

I encourage you to use this book as a tool for self-inquiry and discovery. At the end of each chapter are a series of questions to help you uncover the origins of your own underlying stories.

If you stick with me on this journey, you will be carving a path of freedom. We will get to a place where you will learn how to identify these stories and how to break the hold they have on you. I will leave you with guidance for positive ways to replace the emptiness and loneliness in your heart and how to open and fill your heart in an easy and lasting way that brings fulfillment, connection, comfort, joy, and contentment into your life. Ultimately this will lead you to a life of peace.

Be Free. Be Happy.

Much love,
Pete Caughey

Sanur, Bali, March 2019

TABLE OF CONTENTS

What Are limiting Belief Stories?

Chapter 1

How I Broke Free From Some Of My Stories And Started Seeing The Bigger Picture

One day I was sitting quietly in contemplation and gained a clear insight into some of the things that have happened to me in my life. I saw the physical and emotional limitations I was born with, and I saw clearly the mental and emotional limitations that my parents, schooling, and society had created for me to live in - limitations that were going to make it difficult for me to break free from the way I saw life and the beliefs and stories I had formed. It seemed I had gotten so loaded up that it was going to be difficult to see past my limiting beliefs and grasp the real truth.

Before I was born into this world, I believe I was connected to God's energy, the Oneness or the Source of all things, which I will refer to as Heaven. When I was born, I was still connected to Heaven, but as I grew, I became less and less attached to Heaven's consciousness and became more and more attached to the human world. I believe that I became disconnected from this source, and I also became disconnected from any memory of this feeling of oneness as well. As a fetus inside my mother, I first came into contact with emotions and feelings that my mother was experiencing as well as her reactions, beliefs, and opinions regarding life. Then after I was born, these feelings, emotions, and reactions were confirmed by what I saw, heard, and felt from the people around me, mainly my parents and later on my schooling, community, and society.

I was programmed to be an individual in the world and less connected to God consciousness or the Oneness. Not that anybody did this on purpose. It was just the way it was. I'm not saying my parents weren't connected to God or didn't have a belief in God; I'm saying the things of this world seemed to take a front seat in my learning. I was taught things like how you behaved was important, what was right and wrong, how to speak to people and what to say, what food I should eat and what time I should go to sleep. As I grew up, other things became important like getting a good education, finding a good job, marrying a great wife, having children, buying a house. . . the list goes on and on.

I was not taught about maintaining a connection to something bigger than myself, practicing spiritual gratitude, how to meditate, still the mind or find a place where thoughts don't exist. I wasn't taught about living in the present. I wasn't taught about healthy diets and food. I wasn't taught about understanding emotions and feelings. I wasn't taught about developing deep and intimate relationships with other people, or about loving and accepting others and myself just the way we are, not to have judgments about others and myself, or to love others and myself unconditionally, to have compassion and understanding as to why people act and do the things they do.

No, my life was made a bit more difficult than that. I was brought up believing what other people thought of you was important, wanting people to like you and to think you were a good person, and to worry about how people saw you. I was brought up to believe that having a new car and owning your own home showed you were successful. I had to make some sort of sense out of that. I not only had the so-called normal beliefs and stories of how you are meant to live and survive in the capitalist world, but I also had other things to deal with to make it even harder for me to think I was okay. There seemed to be many things to make me think that there was something wrong with me and that I didn't fit in as I grew up. Each belief may not seem like much individually, but put them all together and it was the making of a very unhappy little boy and later a very unhappy young man with low self-esteem and self-image and a feeling of failure.

What does a person who spent a lot of time trying to make himself feel better about himself do? In the earlier years, I got creative, making tree huts, forts and building rafts to paddle up the river. I climbed high trees so I could look out over the world. Looking back at these things as I write them down, I realize they were all safe places for me to escape from the world I was living in. I was going on adventures away from my family and looking off into the distance where perhaps happiness existed. Maybe that's why I love traveling so much. Maybe in some way, I'm still looking for it, the myth that happiness in somewhere over the rainbow.

Later in my teenage years, I discovered cigarettes, alcohol, drugs, sex and many other addictions that made me feel good. These were things outside of myself to make me feel better inside. I think I was always trying to find somewhere I fit in. Was happiness in the drinking club, the drug-smoking club, or the rugby club? I was in all of these clubs. Nobody ever demonstrated or told me that was not what you do to find happiness and self-acceptance. Hey, that's how my parents and all of my friends around me lived, so why wouldn't it work for me?

What made me change? What woke me up? Well, if I am completely honest, it was when my first wife left me and took my five-year-old son and three-year-old daughter with her. I couldn't understand where I went wrong. I had a great job, wife, two kids, a house, plenty of friends, alcohol, parties, sex, money. I was doing what life told me I should do, and I was successful at it, so what went wrong? What did I miss? What didn't I see? What did I have a blind spot to? It was as if somebody gave me a red pill like in The Matrix. In the movie, the main character Neo has to choose between two pills, a blue pill and a red pill. If he chooses the red pill, he would know the truth and could never go back. It felt like that for me. For the first time, I saw life from a totally different perspective; it was a new life that I had been blind to. I realized all the stories, opinions, and beliefs I held about life may not have necessarily been true. I could see the way I saw myself. The way I needed to prove myself and the way I wanted people to like me. I realized for the first time that I was okay as a child, as a teenager, and as an adult. It was the way I saw life, how I saw myself and what I thought was important that was the problem. I could see how I looked at life and how I was trying to make some sense out of it. I could see how other people were dealing with their lives and the ways they fit into this world. I was good at that version of life. I had created ways to make it work, and I was very busy trying to be perfect.

I can now see that living the way I thought I should wasn't going to work. In that version, I could never really be happy, as I had been set up to fail. I got to see that I could never have enough money because I will always want more. There will always be other people more successful than myself, richer than I am, and happier. This way of life seemed to be designed so that I would always want something or need something. The goal always seemed to be far off in the distance, something to strive for, aspire to, achieve or gain. There was very little contentment or gratitude for who I was or what I already had.

I feel sometimes I was born with many distractions that kept me away from seeing the truth and the real me. I can now say I have broken free from these distractions. I have been able to step back and see the bigger picture. I have choices around this now. Daily I find myself deconstructing and disempowering stories about what I was told life was. This is my personal process of becoming free from those false beliefs.

Exercise 1.

Write your answers in your *Breaking Free* journal.

Title a new page: "I Can See the Truth Behind My Stories Now."

I challenge you to ask where your own opinions and beliefs came from.

1. Ask yourself: Who are you? Where did these beliefs and opinions about yourself come from, and how do you know that they are true?

2. How do you think that you should behave around people? Where did these beliefs and opinions come from, and how do you know they are true?

3. What expectations do you have on how others should behave? Where did you get these expectations from, and how do you know they are true?

4. What are your goals in life and where did they come from? How do you know that's what you are meant to do with your life?

5. What do you think a good relationship should be like and where did you get your ideas about relationships from? How do you know they are true?

Be as honest as you can be answering these questions.

Chapter 2

Why Understanding Someone Else's Story Is Important

I heard what I believe to be a very profound statement in an interview between Tony Robbins and Eben Pagan. Eben is a multi-millionaire and at the end of the interview, Tony asked him what piece of advice he would offer if he could only say one thing. He said, "Have compassion for people, and understand their stories."

I thought this was a fantastic piece of advice. With all of this man's business success, knowledge, experience, and understanding, the number-one piece of advice he gave is the importance of compassion and understanding others. I began to think there could be a life-changing revelation for all of us in his statement.

I believe that to truly have compassion and understanding for others, we need to be aware of a very important point: we are all different. No two people are ever born the same or ever will be. Our individual genetic makeup contains different DNA coding, making us all distinctly unique beings. We like different foods, we go to different schools, and we have different friends. We have different bodies, characters, minds, thoughts, and souls.

Most of the people I have encountered in my life seem to have their own stories about how life is supposed to go; they carry many judgments and opinions about how they and other people should or shouldn't live. Of course, not everybody judges other people, but it appears to me that the thing that blocks true understanding and acceptance of others and ourselves are these judgments and stories. I have certainly fallen victim to judging others and having expectations on how they should lead their lives, but the question is: How can I really judge someone else when their stories and beliefs about life are completely different than mine?

The funny part is that even though I know this, it doesn't stop me from occasionally judging or comparing people. We are an interesting, contrary breed, us humans!

So, now to ask some important questions: What are my stories, where did I get them, and are they really true? What do I think life is all about? What's my moral code? What do I think is okay or not okay? What is my story or views on religion or politics? About money and relationships? Parenting? Where did I get my views from - my parents, teachers, society, friends, or life experiences? I probably got them from all of the above, but which points of view are true? The answer to that is that they are all true for me. The tricky part is that everyone's stories are true for them too, and we may not always agree. Nobody has had the same combination of parents, teachers or experiences that I have, and so ultimately their stories will be different than mine.

This brings us to an even more important question: Is there a real truth, and what is this real truth? Maybe our own stories are our own personal truth in any given moment but are not necessarily the deeper truth of human life and existence on this planet. I encourage you to check the origins of your stories and beliefs, as some of them may have been made up when you were a child or at another time in your life. I don't know if it's reliable to trust the opinions and memories formed by a child with limited life experience and knowledge about what he or she thought might have happened at the time.

By acknowledging we have stories and beliefs that might not necessarily be true, it becomes harder to make judgments about others based on these stories and beliefs. We don't know what experiences and circumstances have occurred in anyone else's life that has shaped their personal truth stories, let alone know why they react to life the way they do.

Exercise 2:

Write your answers in your *Breaking Free* journal.

Title your page: "Understanding My Beliefs."

1. Write a list of subjects that you have strong belief stories around.

   Ask yourself:
   a. What does loyalty mean to you?
   b. What does betrayal mean to you?
   c. What does fear mean to you?
   d. What does being disrespected mean to you?
   e. What does loneliness mean to you?
   f. What does being loved mean to you?

g. What does being accepted by your friends mean to you?

As you have noticed, most of these questions seem to have a negative connotation. In my experience, the negative-based stories have more of an effect and are a bigger driver than positive-based stories in our lives. I encourage you to explore what impact these negative-based stories have had or possibly still are having in your life.

2. Once you have written down your answers to question 1, ask yourself: How do I know if each of these belief stories is true?

3. Where did these belief stories come from?

4. How are these stories stopping or limiting me from fulfilling my true purpose or calling in life?

5. What's a better and more compelling story that I can live by?

Summary

By answering these questions, I have personally uncovered more limiting beliefs and stories that were running in the background that I was not even aware of. Question your stories and beliefs about life and whether or not they are true. Ask yourself if these stories are having a negative impact on your life. If they are, I encourage you to change these stories and create positive, compelling stories to live by, enabling you to lead a more purposeful and satisfying life.

Chapter 3

Are Our Stories True?

Are our stories true? Well, mine are. I think. I have been questioning this, and to be honest, at first I wasn't particularly happy about the result of my inquiry. I have realized that what I think my life is all about and what I think others should and shouldn't do in their lives is not necessarily true; they are just my personal opinions. The truth is that my stories and points of view are only true for me. Seeing life through the lens of my own personal stories, filters, and beliefs has the potential to be limiting. I've also come to the realization that most people are not necessarily going to agree with me because they have their own stories running in the background of how they see life. They have their own beliefs about what is wrong or right for them and what is wrong or right for others. I think that you should all agree with me, so the world will be a better place. *Yeah, right!*

At one of my Taiji School retreats, I was conducting a class on the beach, and I got the participants to walk 20 metres, leaving clear footprints in the sand. Then I got someone else to walk on top of someone else's footprints. I did this myself, and I had a surprising experience. It was like discovering a different aspect of the other person I didn't know, almost like living in someone else's life. I got to experience a bit of their character. It made me think about how differently we all are and how differently we see the world.

We all have different stories, and these stories might not be necessarily be true and are possibly hindering us from living a more expansive life. Stories about money, success, relationships, and happiness. Stories about how parents, family members, children, friends, and lovers should behave. Stories about how business partners, work colleagues, and leaders should conduct themselves. Stories about governments, politics, capitalism, consumerism, education and health systems, religion, and wars and conflict.

So where did I get my stories and viewpoints from? Where did I get my estimation of what a good person should or should not do? Where did I get my idea of how people are supposed to treat each other? In today's modern society, we are heavily influenced by the programming of advertising telling us what we ought to eat, drink, wear, drive, look like, where the most desirable places are to live, and who our friends should be.

I have very strong opinions about the power of advertising and how it manipulates people. They are still just my opinions, and I believe the media and advertising have way too big of an influence on how people see life. I would almost go so far as to say they use mind control techniques or brainwashing to create an image of how the world should be - an image where you are happy and content using their products, the illusion that happiness comes from outside of yourself.

I began to investigate whether the advertising industry is in part responsible for the stories we create and live by. They create an illusionary world where we are influenced into believing that we don't have enough, and that we need to do, be, or buy something to feel fulfilled.

For an example, did you know that the big brands of the fashion industry plan the new fashion styles two years in advance? How do they know what will be in fashion in two years time? Easy. They make it up and tell you what it's going to be. When you buy the clothes that are "in," cleverly designed marketing campaigns tell you it is, and it's not by coincidence that they are the same people who make the clothes.

As members of society, we are encouraged to keep up with the current fashion trends, which are created for us so that you have to keep buying more clothes. Clever marketing terms are used: "This Season's Must-Have Trends" and the "Latest Collections," but what this expertly evokes is that the other side exists as well - that something is "out of style," "not trendy," or "old-fashioned." Tell me who wants to wear something that is out of fashion? Definitely not a teenager. A huge amount of money and advertising targets young women with clothing. I know young women who wouldn't be caught dead in anything without a fashion label on it. I walked through a mall, and I'm sure just about 70% of all of the shops were targeting them. The belief story that has been created for these young women reads something like this: "I'm not okay if I don't wear these current fashion clothes; people won't like me or approve of me; I'm not cool; I may not be accepted by my friends." And this is not restricted to one fashion style. They market to all young women's fashion groups, from preppy to punk, sophisticated, sporty, trashy, edgy, vintage, beachy, rocker, and many more. There is a shop or chain of outlets for all groups and several big name brand stores for each. I know some people don't care about the fashion trends, but you know what I mean. It's a very shrewd example of a self-sustaining business model where the industry dictates what the trends are going to be and then supply them to you.

I think one of the totally absurd things about the fashion industry is that they use ultra tall and thin, size zero women and girls to model their clothes when there are few women in the whole world who look like that. I know that this is changing but the majority of the fashion industry still works this way. Is it their goal to inspire women to look that way? To me, these types of models all look like they need a decent meal, and they definitely don't look healthy. Of course, these are just my opinions. How many women have issues with their weight and size and how they look? How hard has it become for young women and, in fact, all women to simply accept the size and shape of their bodies and not worry about what other people think? So now we have another thriving industry that has started because of this obsession with size and weight. Weight loss programs, weight loss clinics, diets, foods, exercises, liposuction, stomach stapling. How many weight loss formulas are on the market? People seem to have become obsessed with their weight, but why? Both of these industries have made it almost impossible to be content with who you are, and both industries are making a lot of money. These are two stories that feed each other but nevertheless are just made up by society's directed beliefs. Is the story that you have to look a certain way to be accepted so then you will be happy really true? Or are we just being led and told what to believe?

The second example I will use is another great illusion and one I was brought up with - the illusion that going to a particular fast food outlet was a treat. Skillfully designed marketing has brainwashed us into thinking that giving our children unhealthy food is, in fact, a treat. How can giving your children soft drinks full of caffeine and sugar, food coloring, preservatives, and artificial flavorings be regarded as a treat?

Here is another illusionary story. It is a common belief that owning your own home is a major life goal. This story, however, is true typically only for first world countries. Now there is nothing wrong with owning your own home, but what is the true motivation behind this desire? For many people, it is a belief that owning your own home will provide you with security. This story about owning your own home is driven by the banks and lending institutions in order to generate revenue through loan interest and repayments. These lending institutions are interested not in the happiness that this building will provide you and your family - they are interested in being paid interest for 30+ years, which is often more than the value of the house in the first place. It's one of the ways financial institutes make large amounts of money (not that making large amounts of money is a bad thing). Very wealthy people, not countries, own banks. They artfully influence consumers to believe that "Your house will give you security" or "It's an investment" to attract you to borrow money. But I ask you, security from what? Ask any earthquake victims if they feel secure in their homes immediately following an earthquake that flattened their houses and parts of their city? Are they (the banks or the people who own the banks) referring to financial security, such as how much your house is momentarily worth? It is only worth something if you sell it. And if you sell it, where are you going to live?

They could be referring to another form of financial security in that, as you get older, you will have fewer expenses and no rent to pay, but this isn't exactly true either. Running and maintaining a house can be very costly with rates, insurance policies, upkeep, renovation, grounds, and garden maintenance, etc. Another option is to re-mortgage your house to get some money, but that only puts you further into debt and adds more years paying the bank their interest. However, you could own a home and rent it out, and the rent covers the mortgage repayments, rates, insurances, and maintenance, and you may be still left with cash at the end - then you have an asset, not a liability. But if you are living in your own house, that's probably not the case.

I know there are many sound ways of investing to make money out of property; I am just using this as an example to demonstrate that the outside overlying story may be different from the reality.

What about the "living in fear" story? This is about another group of wealthy people who use fear to market and advertise their businesses. "You could lose all of your precious possessions; something could happen to your house; you could have a car accident; someone may steal your camera, so you had better give us large quantities of your money so that we, the insurance companies, can protect you." But when something goes wrong, those same insurance companies will try to find every loophole or clause in the policy so they don't have to pay you. Ask the people in Christchurch, New Zealand how long it took to get money from insurance companies after the earthquakes. I hear that it took one person more than five years to get paid for the damages to her house. I'm not saying all insurance companies are like this but we have all heard of the many cases where this is true. This business model is around keeping people in a constant fear of loss.

My own personal questioning has led me to understand that there are multifaceted sides to every story with different opinions and viewpoints. I would imagine you have your own views on these examples I've given. I'm not even saying that I'm right. They are just my thoughts and ideas, and they are a way to illustrate my point. You are the one who has to wade through all your stories and beliefs about life and come up with what is right for you and what is right to teach your kids. I personally have experienced real value in the ability to see past and question some of my own personal stories that were and are fed to me. I'm now not so fixed in my beliefs. I question my belief's validity, and I encourage you to do the same.

The question that I ask myself is: How many other belief stories do I have running in the background that are based on illusions I have accepted from advertisers? Since inquiring into these beliefs every day, my life has become richer, and I feel more aware and wiser knowing the origins of these stories. It has helped me see the world though judicious eyes.

Exercise 3:

Write your answers in your *Breaking Free* journal.

Title your page: "Identifying Your Belief Stories."

I have outlined questions below to evoke a practice inquiring into the stories that you may have around why you like the things you do.

1. Which model and make of car do you like and why?

   Example answer: I like M3 BMW's cars because I want to be seen in a quality European car with quality German engineering. The M3 is the sports model so the image that I associate with this car is I am a person who likes quality. I have enough money to buy expensive cars. I like exhilaration. I like adventure, and I'm still young at heart to have fun in a sports car. Having one of these cars would make me feel successful. (This is not actually what I think or what I believe all BMW owners think. It's an example of how you could answer this question.)

2. What fast food outlets do you like and why?

3. What clothing shops do you like and why?

4. What supermarket do you shop at and why?

5. What image is associated with these?

6. What feelings does the association with these evoke?

Summary

These are just a few examples of stories that have an outside face, an apparent truth, but underneath have a different reality. My goal in this book is to help you see your own stories, how to unlock them and understand the truth behind them so that you can become liberated from them. We also have an array of emotional and relationship stories with underlying stories running through them as well. During this book, we will uncover other stories about relationships, religion, spirituality, money, parenting, and many more topics. I will give you insight into what I think may be the underlying stories associated with your point of views, opinions, and beliefs.

One of the most useful sayings I use while helping people to uncover their stories is: It's not what you do, it's why you do it. And to use my favourite catch phase, "Let the truth set you free."

Chapter 4

What's The Problem?

I was brought up to think that problems are negative, but as an adult, I have found myself questioning if this idea is true. The time when I had the most problems was also the time when I had the most rewarding growth. I'm not suggesting that you consciously welcome problems into your life; instead, I am suggesting that you consciously choose to observe the problem and respond in a more positive way than you may have in the past.

Imagine a world without problems: the perfect job, perfect partner, perfect kids, the perfect life. The novelty of this would be satisfying for a while, but then guess what would happen? Boredom. Even if you were happy with everything in your life being the status quo, I believe eventually you would get bored because we all have a need for a certain degree of uncertainty in our lives. If everything was that perfect in my life, it would drive me insane. Heavens, I'm a man; I wouldn't have anything to fix, no problems to solve. As I say, it may be okay for a while, but for me, it would eventually drive me crazy!

In life, there seems to be several stages toward reaching the resolution of a problem, starting with the identification of the problem to finding a solution, the growth stage, and then change, which in turn creates more problems. And so it seems to go on. I think the key is to create quality problems. A quality problem is having a positive approach to a problem instead of a negative one.

An example of a typical problem could be having a job you don't like. Seeing it as a quality problem would be deciding to look for a new job and having to choose all the new and exciting job possibilities that you'd like to do and then have fun applying for them. Another example of creating a quality problem could be leaving an unfavorable relationship; a quality problem could be finding a new exciting, loving, and fulfilling relationship. If you had to move from your house, a quality problem could be finding a more comfortable, warmer, and beautiful house. If the problem were that you had to confront or communicate with someone who is difficult to talk to, the quality problem would be coming up with empowering, positive, and resourceful ways to communicate with them.

At first, it can be challenging to train ourselves to see the possible positive aspects of a problem, but maybe a starting point could be by asking the following questions:

- *How can I see this problem differently?*
- *How can I see all the different ways in which I could resolve this problem?*
- *What are the positive aspects that could be gained by resolving this problem?*
- *How can I make it a "quality" problem?*
- *Why has this problem arisen in the first place, and what is the lesson I can learn from it?*

To change the way you view problems, focus on the positive aspect of the problem and its positive outcome by making them quality problems.

Maybe it is the solution that is the problem, as we may not like the way our problems need to be to be resolved? An example of this could be if you're in a job that you don't like and it is stressful, but you don't want to go through the process of finding another job.

A problem for me, which turned out to be a major growth opportunity, was that I was unable to ask someone for help. I had a limiting belief that if you ask someone for help, it's a sign of weakness and incompetence by not being able to do it yourself. I changed this belief because I realized that this wasn't true and that other people like to help people, and that if others helped me, it wasn't a sign of my incompetence. I also discovered that other people have skills I don't have. By looking at problems as an opportunity to grow, it becomes an advantageous problem. I now have no problem asking people for help, and there is a certain sense of freedom that accompanies this.

I have also identified what I have termed as "safe problems." These are problems within our control like depression, anxiety, and stress. It is possible that some people may read this and think you don't have control over depression and anxiety, but I would like to challenge that idea. It is my belief that we always have a choice, no matter how hard it may seem. I have personally experienced depression, and at the time it felt there was no way out. I found myself saying, "If there is a way in, there has to be a way out." I believe it's the stories running in the background that are most of the problem as well as the belief that we're not meant to have any problems. Stories like not being loved, not being good enough, not being heard, not feeling significant, not feeling useful, not feeling noticed, not feeling respected, not feeling attractive. The stories of failure go on and on. But they are still just stories, despite how real they may seem.

I have treated many people with depression. I have heard their stories, and on some occasions, they just don't want to let the story go because who would they be without it? It's a great question, and my answer is: they would be free. I know of people who are depressed, and all they talk about is everything that is wrong with the world, wrong with themselves, and wrong with their lives. It gives them something to talk about. It can help them validate their stories and problems while making them feel significant. But this isn't always the case. Sometimes these stories are about safety and significance. I don't want to undermine the severity of these illnesses or claim that I have all the answers. I am just saying that there is always something you can do about it.

One of the most powerful examples of transforming a problem into a quality problem is the incarceration of Nelson Mandala. Nelson Mandala spent 27 years in prison; however, he remained a free man due to his mindset and focus on his purpose of ending apartheid in South Africa. He used his time in jail to prepare for the time when he was released. And when he was released, it was evident that only love existed in his heart despite the injustice that was bestowed on him throughout his lifetime.

Other "safe problems" can be procrastination, food, drugs, alcohol, and addictions, hesitation, blaming others for your troubles, withdrawing from relationships, just to name a few. "Safe problems" seem to be safe and not so much of a big deal. They can be keeping us from emotions and the feelings we are trying to avoid. Yet, these so-called "safe problems" can be causing more pain and hardship than quality problems. Sometimes we will create a "safe problem" that covers up a problem that we don't have control over. For example, people who drink alcohol instead of dealing with a quality problem such as not being happy in a relationship.

I choose to see problems as a gift - the gift to discover what lies behind them. I believe problems can provide us with an opportunity to step into our personal power and create change and movement in our lives. Problem-solving involves stepping up and getting out of our comfort zones. Problem-solving can engage and evoke one to excel. It can initiate courage, determination, great thought processes, self-discovery, willpower, bravery, and creativity. It can also resolve, call you to speak your truth, and be seen. These all seem like pretty good outcomes to me.

Pushing through the resistance to the problem may seem to be a bit of a challenge, but it builds character. It builds muscles: mental, emotional and spiritual muscles. So roll on the quality problems, roll on the growth, roll on the adventure, and roll on the freedom!

Exercise 4.

Write your answers in your *Breaking Free* journal.

Title your new page: "Creating Quality Problems."

1. Think of a problem you have right now.

2. Think of how you could change it into a quality problem.

   For example:
   a. **Problem:** I don't have enough money to pay the bills.
   Quality problem: What are all the creative and fun ways I can create money to pay the bills?

   b. **Problem:** My wife says I don't spend enough time with her.
   Quality problem: What are new and exciting ways that I can spend time with my wife and do something we have never done before?

Summary

I encourage you to change your perspective around problem-solving and instead turn the problems into quality problems. Sometimes it is as easy as seeing the problems from a different perspective and accepting that problems are a normal part of life.

Change the way you see your problems, and it will change your life.

Chapter 5

How Do You Defend Yourself From Feeling Your Biggest Emotional Pain?

There are many different methods we use to avoid experiencing a feeling we don't like, which in my experience is often driven by our personal thought patterns. Thoughts like, "Nobody really loves me," or "I'm not good enough," "Nobody really wants to listen to me," or "I don't have anything important to say" - these thoughts more often than not result in feelings of inadequacy or a feeling that there is something wrong with you. You may identify with some of the above and other thought patterns won't have relevance to you, but generally, we have thoughts and feelings running in the background that are influencing our emotional life. Discovering these feelings is the key to emotional freedom.

Some of the common methods people use to avoid feeling the pain that comes from these thoughts vary, from withdrawing from people and situations that appear to be causing the pain at an external level, closing down internally to protect yourself, or expressing anger toward people who are triggering the feeling in you either through what they say or do. Another method is finding fault in people, judging and making them feel "bad" to make yourself feel better. Or, you may even transfer or redirect the attention to somebody else and point out that what they are doing is not right, taking the attention off yourself in order to avoid feelings of pain, rejection, or inadequacy.

If you use the transferring or redirecting method to avoid your own feelings of discomfort, you may use comments like, "But you do that," or "You say things like that," or "You speak terribly to me, which is why I react the way I do," or "When I ask you to stop, you don't listen to me." All of these responses can be ways of redirecting attention from yourself so you don't have to be responsible for your own feelings and discomfort.

Notice all of these comments use the word "You." For example, "You do this" and "You always do that," or "I see you doing that," or "You are not listening to me," or "You don't give me time to speak." These statements contain very little responsibility in owning one's own feelings and reactions.

Perhaps a more helpful and empowering way to deal with the uncomfortable feelings could be to use the "I" language and say, "I am feeling uncomfortable when you say that," "I'm feeling angry towards you," "I'm feeling inadequate," "I feel unsafe," or "I feel vulnerable," "I feel out of control," "I notice there is a large resistance to not wanting to hear what you are saying right now," "I am feeling threatened," "I feel nervous," and so on. At first, these words may seem to be coming from a place of weakness or disempowerment, but the truth is quite the contrary. They are words of immense honesty, courage, and strength and are an incredibly powerful step in taking self-responsibility and breaking down stories that could be holding you back.

I find another powerful tool is to be curious about your reactions and resistances. To look at why there is a charge around a subject, person, or situation can lead to key revelations about stories you have running in the background. So I encourage you to be curious about why you do the things you do and about the things you react to.

I believe the subject or situation you have the biggest reaction to, the biggest charge, the biggest reluctance and the thing you are most unwilling to explore could potentially be the one thing that is stopping your biggest growth and biggest breakthrough. It may also be the thing you will defend the most and have possibly built the biggest defensive wall around. You will find all sorts of ways of not going there. You may not even know you are defending it, let alone know what you are defending. You will know where it is though. It's the one you get the angriest about when you feel other people are backing you into a corner, when you feel threatened or uncomfortable.

I believe it is useful to ask yourself, "What am I defending?" and "What am I defending myself from?" Or is it that you are really trying to protect yourself from an unwanted feeling that you will do almost anything not to feel and at all costs?

This feeling is very real and could be your biggest fear, a fear that you might be found out, that you're not the person you want people to see you to be. Maybe if they found out, people wouldn't like you; they may think you are a fraud. You may have a fear that people might find out that you don't know as much you as you want people to think you know.

There are many reasons we unconsciously choose to defend our position. My own example of this stems from my childhood. As a young boy, I struggled with reading and spelling. I thought there was something wrong with me, and I didn't want people to find out because I thought I was dumb. I carried a huge amount of embarrassment as a result. I built up coping methods around this, and if anybody said I couldn't read very well, I made up excuses. I developed great ways of blaming other people for it. But most of all, I would just hide away and hoped that no one would ever find out. Later on, I found out that I was dyslexic. However, as a child, I just thought something was wrong with me. Nobody told me that being dyslexic was the reason why my brain seemed to be dysfunctional. At that time there wasn't very much information about dyslexia or learning disabilities.

Later in life, I developed other ways to avoid the feeling of inadequacy. I started getting angry if my secret was threatened, and further on I noticed the anger turned into rage. However, I become curious and began a deep inquiry as to where this rage was coming from, and I have subsequently carried out processes and inquiry work around this, which has resulted in major personal breakthroughs. I realized that my dyslexia was a gift, and it made me use my mind in a unique way, which allowed me to develop other highly useful skills and strengths and has made me the person I am today.

Another way I used to avoid feelings of inadequacy was to play the victim. I tried everything I could to get people to give me sympathy. I would say, "I'm just doing my best," and "I'm trying," or "I just don't understand." Later on, I got to see that all of this was a manipulation to get people to think that I'm a good person and to feel sorry for me, thereby keeping me from taking responsibility.

I see very clearly now that these behaviors and habits are just defenses to help me avoid the feelings of pain and discomfort that stem from my vulnerability and inadequacy. I know the true meaning of this story now, and it is quite different to what I tricked myself into believing for many years. It was a revelation when I finally saw the truth behind my childhood stories of thinking I was dumb and that there was something wrong with me.

As a result of not being able to read and write very well, I developed other skills including my ability to communicate verbally and use my senses. I not only developed my ability to express myself thoughtfully and mindfully, but over the years, I've learned how to hear people - not only hear what they are saying but to hear what they really mean behind their words and what they are not saying. Today this is a valuable strength in being able to understand and communicate honestly with my patients. It helps me to understand more clearly what has brought about their illness and discomfort. I see it as an incredible gift, which may not have developed had I not experienced limitations around reading and writing as a child. The result of what appeared as a major failure and handicap as a child has given me one of my biggest blessings, and I now have immense gratitude for this.

Exercise 5.

Write your answers in your *Breaking Free* journal.

Title your new page: "How Do I Defend Myself?"

1. What are some of the ways you defend yourself if you feel vulnerable or challenged?

2. What is the underlying belief or story you are defending?

3. What apparent disadvantages in your life have turned out to be positive advantages?

Summary

I encourage you to become curious the next time you catch yourself defending a story that makes you feel inadequate. I invite you to check out your underlining story and any fears that you have created around it. This could be the story that lives behind your anger and frustrations. These feelings might just be the doorway to your biggest earth-shattering discoveries about yourself that could help set you free.

Inquire into and to be curious anytime you get angry, frustrated, judgmental, or defensive to discover the stories and the feelings that come with such revelations.

How To Identify
Your Stories

Chapter 6

Do We Have A Negative Default Setting?

Do we have a negative default setting similar to a computer's default setting? Is our default setting programmed to see what is wrong instead of what is right? I remember my son saying to me one day, "Why is it so hard to be good and so easy to be bad?" In the world, this seems to be true with the amount of wars, violence, corruption, stealing, betrayal, lies, hatred, and judgment. I'm not saying there aren't great things being done also, as there certainly are. I'm just asking, why do we revert back to seeing what is wrong in our world, especially in times of stress?

When I buy a car, I go and have a look at it, and all I notice and search for are the things that are wrong with it. Do I pick my partners the same way, noticing their faults and not what is wonderful about them? When I buy a house, what do I look at? When a sports team loses, do we focus on what they did right or wrong?

The TV news focuses mainly on negative events. The opposing party focuses on what is going wrong with the governing political party. In modern western medicine, most of the focus is on fixing or healing the sick, not on how to maintain good health. The way we think does affect our health, according to a post, "How to Trick Your Brain for Happiness," on the Berkley University website *Greater Good Magazine* by Rick Hanson, a Neuropsychologist, founder of the Wellspring Institute for Neuroscience and Contemplative Wisdom, and *New York Times* best-selling author. He says, "People who routinely experience chronic stress release the hormone cortisol, which literally eats away at the hippocampus, which is a part of the brain that's very engaged in visual-spatial memory as well as memory for context and setting."

The more cortisol that's released in response to negative experiences and thoughts, the more difficult it can become over time to form new positive memories. This can, in turn, make it more difficult to see positive things that are happening in our lives right now.

How can we shift our focus to what is right with life? How do we stay focused on the great, magnificent, and wonderful things, and not on what is going wrong? How do we see the glass as half full and not half empty?

In the same article, Hanson says that humans are evolutionarily wired with a negativity bias. I wonder, is this a primal survival mechanism? Maybe in the early stages of the development of the human race, we focused on what we needed to survive, not on the abundance of what we already had. The primary focus was on needing food. Maybe because of this default setting, we still focus on what we want and need from a survival perspective.

In the western world, it seems we are not content with the basics: food, clean water, warmth, clothes, and shelter. We live in a society where commercialism is king - a bottomless pit of wanting rare exotic foods, stylish clothes, bigger houses, fancy appliances, greater technology, and luxurious holidays. Will we ever reach a place of contentment with what we already have? Why do we want more and more and sometimes feel like a failure if we do not achieve what we think we should have? When do we arrive at the end of the goal? What does "better off" look like? I have talked to many parents who say their kids want everything and expect to get it. How did we create this society of always wanting something? When do the kids become content and happy with what they have, and what are our responsibilities around teaching the new generations to feel this way?

The negative default settings seem to be more prevalent in certain occupations, relationships, and conversations. I have noticed that I can start having a conversation, and before long we are talking about what is wrong with life! Or the weather, kids of today, how expensive everything is, how some countries are treating each other, and so on. But now, I consciously choose to stop that negative talk and instead focus on the positive aspects of the world, what is positive about people, relationships, and especially what is positive about myself. Tony Robbins says, "What you focus on is where your energy flows," and Traditional Chinese Medicine says, "Where the mind goes the Qi goes."

My internal computer asked me, "Do you want to change your default setting to another browser?" I clicked "Yes" to a new browser that only has positive, uplifting, and motivating sites displayed. The world, its people, and I look very different in this browser. Then I need to remember to put all the old files in the recycle bin and delete them, or they may reappear!

Summary

Feed the good feelings, not the bad feelings.
The ones you water are the ones that grow.
The feelings you focus on are where your energy goes.

I believe that to make significant shifts, we need to keep affirming the positive every day, twice a day, three times a day... as many times as you need. Remember the old default setting has been there for the majority of your life, and it's not likely to give up easily. I believe we need to beat it to death with positivity or the default settings will come back; they may be that big in our subconscious.

Our minds may have a more significant affect on the health of our body than we think. Focus on the positive! Thinking negative thoughts may be releasing stress hormones, which will hurt you on many levels, and the energy and vibration of these thoughts may even be creating illness in your body.

Focus on the positive, see all the good things that you have in your life, see the positive in other people and yourself, and have gratitude for what you've already got.

Chapter 7

Are People Mirrors Of Us?

There are many teachings about how other people are simply a reflection of ourselves and how we can see ourselves, both our negative and positive aspects, through other people. If we see things in other people we don't like, then this is a great indication there are parts of ourselves we don't like or are unwilling to accept. The theory is that if we have a judgment on someone else's actions, it is because we have a judgment on ourselves for the same actions, which we still do or we used to do. It can be a pretty confronting idea that any time I see something in someone else I don't like, they are mirroring something I don't like or accept in myself. There could be exceptions to this, as others may have behaviors or characteristics that we dislike or make a judgment of, and it is not necessarily apart of our own character but a reflection of our own beliefs or stories. Becoming aware of our reactions and judgments is not only useful in discovering our own true character but also the stories we have about how others should behave.

I personally have found this to be true, and I see it as a great way to discover deeper unconscious layers of myself. It also allows me to witness myself from a different perspective. This can be painful sometimes, as I would like to think that I'm not like the people I am judging. The truth is that I could be seeing an aspect about myself that I don't necessarily like or that I am being triggered by another's actions, which I have a judgment about. Being able to accept that I am doing this is hard yet incredibly rewarding and enlightening. I have many examples of this concept transpiring in my life and would like to share a couple of instances.

I have witnessed many ways people utilize different techniques to gain attention, love, significance, and understanding in their lives, and at some level, I believe we all crave these attributes. I certainly have been no exception to this rule. I found myself being particularly judgmental about people who seemed to talk constantly about themselves, all the time, with seemingly little interest for what was going on in another's life. I found this personality type to be very needy because it was always about them. The reason this triggered me so intensely in the past is that, yes, you guessed it, I did it and still do to a certain extent. I didn't like the fact that I talked at length about myself, so ultimately I didn't like people who I perceived behave in this way. Ultimately, it held up a mirror that I had to face within myself.

I can trace this trigger back to an experience I had as a child. When I was a kid, I was bright, bubbly and happy, laughing most of the time. I was a bit of a character, so I've been told. I made people laugh with my humor and antics. I worked out that you get attention when you do this; you get noticed, and that made me feel good. And then I started getting comments from my parents saying things like, "Don't be a show off" and "Who do you think you are?" I was a very confident child, but my mother saw it as cocky behavior and would put me down, a case of the tall poppies syndrome. As a result, I started talking myself up because nobody else did. When you have low self-esteem, everybody says to you, "Well done; you're fantastic; you can do it; you are doing really well." But when you are really confident, people have a tendency to say nothing. So then people like me do one of two things: they either start playing up to get attention or they'll do what I did, which was to start telling people about how good I was. The ironic part about this is that some people would start putting me down, so I talked myself up a little more, and the cycle continued right into adulthood.

We all know people who do this, and it is likely that you will experience one of two reactions to this person. One, you will accept this person, who they are, and have compassion for their pain, or you will judge them and decide you don't like them. Now if we go back to the start of this chapter, you will remember that if you have a judgment on someone, it's likely because there is a part of you that doesn't like this characteristic and hasn't accepted it in yourself. If you are willing to fully acknowledge and accept it in yourself and love yourself despite your perceived flaws, then it's possible you will have no reaction to this type of behavior.

Initially, this was a hard pill to swallow. I have accepted this behavior in myself, but I still catch myself doing it from time to time. Now I accept that at those times I might have been feeling the need for attention. When I acknowledge this, the need to talk about myself to gain attention seems to melt away.

Another one of my persistent judgments is I don't like people who talk all the time (in general), and yes, it's because I like to talk a lot. Again, this story began in my childhood. As a young boy, I felt nobody really listened to me. I never felt heard. I was brought up in a culture where "children should be seen and not heard."

Because I liked communicating a lot, I was put down for talking too much. As a result, I would look for situations where I could talk and people would listen. I became a leader of groups, a captain of teams, a teacher, and a therapist.

I was talking to one of my Taiji teachers once and he asked me, "Why do you want people to like you?"

I answered, "Because I'm a good person."

He said, "Yes, you are, but there will always be people who won't like you."

"Why not?" I replied.

"For one reason, you talk a lot."

"Well, I will stop talking so much!" I said.

He replied, "Then you wouldn't be yourself anymore."

This valuable and extremely kind lesson has taught me about accepting myself for myself. The acknowledgment of it has also allowed my love for talking to be expressed in different forms, for example in this book you are reading. I love to write because ultimately I love to communicate. Acknowledging this in myself allows me to accept other people who are also big talkers! This has also enabled me to become a better listener.

I now see and focus on the good parts of people. It's easy to see faults or things that we think we could improve on both in ourselves and in other people. I believe that looking at the positive aspects of others and ourselves is a much more empowering way to live. This does not mean that the other aspects do not exist. My belief is: what you feed is what will grow.

Now if I find I have a negative reaction or trigger to someone else's behavior, I know it is an opportunity to discover another aspect of myself that I haven't yet accepted, or it is one of my stories that I have a judgment around regarding other people's behavior. Understanding that the behavior of others is a mirror of my own behavior has helped me to become less judgmental and have more understanding, love, and acceptance. It has also allowed me to break free from some behavioral patterns and stories that have bound me to my past.

Exercise 6.

Write your answers in your *Breaking Free* journal.

Title your new page: "People Are Mirrors Of Our Own Stories."

1. Think of some of the people in your life whom you don't like. What is it that you don't like about them?

2. Can you recognize these behaviors or qualities in yourself?

3. Think about some of the people whom you admire and love; what are the qualities that you love about them? Do you recognize these qualities in yourself?

Chapter 8

Driven By Not Wanting To Feel
A Negative Emotion

Sometimes I notice myself not wanting to feel a negative emotion. Other times I don't realize that a negative emotion is driving my thoughts, my reactions, and my speech. I will add at this time that I don't think any emotions are actually negative or positive; they are just different feelings in the body. Like notes on a keyboard, there are no good or bad notes - just varying frequencies and vibrations. Most of us have been told at an early age that some emotions are good, like happiness, and some are bad, like anger. I challenge this belief, but for the purposes of this chapter, we will continue using "positive" and "negative" phrasing to distinguish emotions.

My ego seems to find comfort in these so-called negative emotions even though I know I would prefer to feel a positive emotion. My good friend Chris explained his thoughts on negative emotions to me one day. He believes that negative thoughts provide a place of comfort even though they may be negative. And this negative energy provides a false sense of security. I notice from personal experience that when I want to be happy, I am driven more by the fact that I don't want to feel sad. This sounds like a strange thing to say, and I have discovered the real reason that drives me is not always what it appears to be. Even more crazy is that I will sit in this strangely comfortable feeling of negativity when negative feelings are also the feelings we will do anything not to feel.

Tony Robbins says that people will do anything to avoid feeling the pain of negative emotions, and it is a key driving factor for most people. I found this a difficult concept to understand initially, but it makes sense after looking at my own life and seeing how this concept has played out. I remember when I was younger, I wanted people to like me, so I used to purposefully set out to please people until they would. I wasn't really driven by wanting people to like me; I was driven by the fact that I didn't want to feel unloved. This is the same with money. Quite often I am driven to make more money not because of the feeling of joy of feeling abundant, but because of the feeling that comes from not having any money. And in my case, the feeling of emptiness, the fear of failure, and the fear of not being successful play a factor. The problem with this is that if you are driven by not wanting to feel a negative feeling, then by the Law of Attraction, you will attract the very thing you don't want. If what is driving you is the fear of lack of money, then what you will create is more lack of money or more fear as that is what you are focusing on. Remember, "Where your focus goes, your energy flows."

Sometimes this negative feeling is what gets people out of bed in the morning to go to work. It's not because they want to go to work but because of what it would feel like if they didn't. How can we change this? Of course, the obvious answer is to do things for a "positive" reason - make money because you want to feel the joy of financial freedom, for example. I have also observed that this also comes up with matters of love. Sometimes I want to feel loved, but it seems to be driven more by not wanting to experience the feeling of being unloved. Being unloved is one of the worst feelings in the world, and this has been proven with babies who were born and abandoned by their mothers in orphanages and who did not experience love at a crucial time in their lives. Some of these children may not have thrived or even survived. In contrast, the children who were loved and held every day thrived and survived. It is a natural need of every human being to feel loved and nurtured. It is difficult then when you want to be needed and loved by somebody because that will give the power to someone else on how you feel. So perhaps the key is to love yourself while removing any expectations that others should love you.

An interesting question to ask yourself when you catch yourself performing certain behavioral patterns is, "What is my motivation?" and "Why am I doing this right now?" Sometimes the answer is not what it appears to be. I believe that the ability to understand our actions makes us more conscious and aware of our behavioral patterning, which gives us clear signposts as to why we do the things we do. Awareness gives us a certain type of freedom and is a step closer to knowing our true selves. I encourage you to look at your actions and know what the driving motivators are. This will allow you to make more conscious choices.

Exercise 7.

Write your answers in your *Breaking Free* journal.

Title a new page: "I Am Motivated By Positive Feelings."

Ask yourself these questions and write down your answers:

1. What emotions will you do anything to avoid feeling? For example, sadness, anger, rage.

2. What are feelings you don't like? For example, anger, frustration, feeling vulnerable, feeling out of control, feeling weak, feeling financially broke, feeling lonely, feeling worthless, feeling unheard, feeling betrayed, feeling disrespected, feeling that no one likes you.

3. What do you do to avoid feeling these feelings? For example, do you work more and keep yourself busy, do you eat comfort foods, go shopping, watch TV or movies, drink alcohol, take recreational drugs, eat chocolate, go to the gym, go for a run, talk to your friends? What do you do to avoid feeling these very uncomfortable feelings?

4. What are some of the emotions that drive you? Is it out of a need for happiness, a need to be loved, a need to be liked, a need to be valued? (And any other ones you can think of.)

Note:
Bring the feelings that you avoid experiencing to the surface. By becoming aware of such feelings, it empowers you. Writing them down enables you to break the cycle and begin the healing process.

Chapter 9

The Yin Yang Theory

The Yin Yang is a multi-faceted subject with many aspects. I want to bring attention to just one part of this theory to help us understand the concept of duality. I think most people understand the ideas of Yin Yang as opposites, like day and night, up and down, male and female, for example. But that is a common misconception. Yin and Yang can be more accurately described as two parts of one whole. For example, females and males are the two parts that make up the human race. The heads side of a coin is one side while tails is the other, and together they make up a single coin. If we introduce the concept of right and wrong, then the whole piece must be a combination of both right and wrong. If we have something that is wrong, then automatically a right must exist as well. The question is, wrong and right to what? What is the piece in the middle that they are measured by? What is the whole, and what are they on either side of?

I want to pick an example, but it is very difficult to choose one without triggering any of your own thoughts, beliefs, opinions, or stories on the subject. Let's try using the example of getting married. Some people have strong viewpoints about living together with someone in a romantic partnership, that you need to be married first, while some people think it is okay to live together with someone and not be married. As we know, there are many different opinions and beliefs around this subject and even beliefs about which one is right and which one is wrong. The truth is, they are just beliefs about a single core subject, which is two people living together. The piece in the middle is that most often two humans who love each other choose to live with each other and want to share their lives together.

Another common example is that people may think that there is the right food to eat and the wrong food to eat, but the whole story is about food itself. Good weather or bad weather ultimately is still two aspects of weather. I can almost hear your minds ticking over! How about the perception that there is a right way and a wrong way to raise children? What about the right or the wrong way to take a photo? The right way or the wrong way to park your car? Consider that parenting is just parenting, and a photo is just a photo, and that parking cars is just parking cars. Ultimately there is no right or wrong way; it is just our own individual opinion and viewpoints.

I am using the wrong and right comparison of the Yin Yang theory as it is commonly used to illustrate different points of view and opinions. Are our opinions just our stories of what we think is right, and our judgments are what we think is wrong? Is the bigger picture to say, "It is just what it is" and "Things are just what they are?" Is it our beliefs, opinions, and judgments that take us away from our ability to see the whole picture?

It is just one day of our lives - it isn't daytime or nighttime. People generally don't ask, "Did you have a good daytime yesterday?" They ask, "Did you have a good day?" which includes day and night. There isn't a good hug and a bad hug; they are just hugs that are different from one another. Unless you have a judgment on what a bad hug is or an opinion of what a good hug should be, then they are both just your point of view. Is it necessary to distinguish between the two? Can you let your opinion or judgments go and see them as different kinds of hugs? Are our stories and opinions just Yin Yang beliefs?

The main point that I want to bring to your attention is how Yin and Yang influences our mental and emotional lives. Our emotional world seems to be defined by duality and the contrast of these two Yin and Yang aspects. We learn about the emotional world through these duality contrasts. We learn about relationships, people whom we like and people we dislike, the actions of people we agree with and actions we disagree with. We learn from the dual relationships with ourselves, what we like about ourselves and what we don't like. I believe it is a diversion and a disempowering trap we can get caught in when we see emotions from one side, view something as right or as wrong, or as positive or negative. For example, having a judgment on someone's behavior as being unacceptable, such as somebody not saying "Thank you" after you have given them something, can trap you in the feeling of not being appreciated. The other side of the story could be that the person doesn't like receiving gifts and was embarrassed and didn't know what to say. Both of these stories have their own Yin and Yang component. You may not care if people say "Thank you" or not; it's just that you like giving, or the other side could be that they love receiving gifts, and it makes them feel appreciated. The bigger picture of this interaction and what transpired may be something completely different to both of these two different sides of the exchange. The big picture is that it is part of the giving and receiving cycle, which is a fundamental principle of the universe. You water a plant and it grows, night turns into day, and day turns into night. It is the cyclic concept of life and death and there is no end - it keeps revolving. But we can get caught up in the smaller details called points of view or opinion and beliefs.

So when we get stuck in a Yin or Yang belief such as "They didn't say thank you," or "I feel unappreciated," then we get stuck in one side of duality and we lose sight of the bigger picture, thereby limiting ourselves from our true potential and vision.

We live in a world of duality and opposites, or Yin and Yang. How can we learn about the world through these opposites and not get caught on one side or the other? When we have different viewpoints, opinions, and beliefs, we can create and get locked into the wrong and right, good and bad, happy and sad duality concepts. We have been programmed to think the head side of the coin is better than the tail side, that "yes" is better than "no," that the Queen of Hearts is better than the Queen of Spades, that a green traffic light is better than a red light, on is better than off, heaven is better than hell, right-handed people are normal and left-handed people are not, sweet is a better taste than sour, feeling good is better than feeling down, holidays are better than working, rich is better than poor, slim is better than fat, educated people are better than uneducated people. Some of these you may think there is no difference, but others may have strong opinions about them. What if none of these ideas are true and the truth is that they are all just different, not one better than the other?

I encourage you to question your opinions and their origins and to see the bigger picture. Look at the whole coin, not just the heads side. Look at the whole elephant, not just its ears and trunk. Look at the whole person, not just what they are wearing. Look at the whole person, not just their behavior. Yin Yang is a way of describing a concept of separation, a division of the whole into two parts. Yin Yang in the human world has created separation not only in people and beliefs but also in societies, communities, and in countries. It has created separations in politics, religious beliefs, and in gender. I believe creating harmony in the world is by joining the two pieces back together, seeing the one piece, seeing a whole person, seeing a whole community, seeing a whole country, seeing all of humanity, seeing all of nature, by seeing the whole world and the whole earth.

Exercise 8.

Write your answers in your *Breaking Free* journal.

Title your new page: "All Stories Have Two Sides."

> 1. Write a list of beliefs you have about what is right and wrong ways for people to behave.
>
>   For example:
>   a. It is right to be loyal and it is wrong to be disloyal?
>   b. It is right to be generous and it is wrong to be mean?
>   c. It is right to be honest and it is wrong to be dishonest?
>
> 2. Write a list of beliefs you have about good and bad.

For example:

   a. Honest people are good; dishonest people are bad.
   b. Happy, respectful people are good; angry, disrespectful people are bad.
   c. Good people use rubbish bins; bad people litter.
   d. Good people are courteous on the roads; bad people drive aggressively on the roads.

3. If you have trouble writing these lists, try writing a list of what you think "good" people do and how they behave. When you finish this list, write a list of opposite behaviors that identify what "bad" people do.

Summary

Look at your lists. You may be surprised to see how many opinions you have about other people's behaviors. Where did you get these opinions? Who told you they were true?

Do you really know what is going on with all these people? Do you know how they have suffered in their lives or know the hardships they have experienced? Do we know what their parents were like and the kind of upbringing they had? Do you really know what has made them behave this way - a way you may think is wrong? Do you really know what has made this person to be this way, without using generalizations?

It is easy to have these opinions and judgments on other people. Society is quick to point the finger and judge people on their behavior, and society is quick to condemn so-called wrong behavior. Wouldn't it be more valuable to seek the source of the problem and find a solution than to have a judgment? I do know many people in the world spend their lives trying to resolve the social problems of the world, and my sincere respect goes to these people. Where do we get these wrong and right opinions from? Who made them up? Is there a good set of ethical and moral rules that we as humans should live by? They seem to be made up from the belief of right and wrong, good and bad people, happy and sad people, kind people and selfish people, rich people and poor people.

There is a great example of a tribe in Africa who handles the issues of "right" and "wrong" differently. If someone in the tribe performs a perceived wrong action, they are put in the middle of the tribe and everyone acknowledges them.

SAWABONA STORY

On their website, the Sawabona Association writes:

"Members of the northern Natal tribes of South Africa have a beautiful tradition. When a member of the tribe does something harmful and wrong, they take that person to the centre of the village and the whole tribe surrounds him. For two days, they tell that person all good things he has done to each one of them.

The tribe believes that every human being comes into the world as a good being, and in the pursuit of happiness, love, peace and security, people make mistakes. The tribe sees those mistakes as a scream for help. They unite to lift that person and to reconnect him to his true nature, which he had been temporarily disconnected.

The members greet each other by saying 'Sawabona,' which literally means 'I see you' as a way to say, 'I respect you, I value you, you are important to me.' In response, people say 'Sikhona,' which means, 'I am here; I exist for you.'

This tradition acknowledges the connection that we share as human beings and our gratitude to one another by saying, 'Until you see me, I do not exist,' and 'When you see me, you bring me into existence.'" (SawabonaAssociation.com).

What does the big picture look like when there is no right and wrong, no judgments, no Yin and Yang, no duality? Where there is acknowledgment that we are all just people trying to make some sense of the chaos in the world? Where some people live a life of luxury with all the money and food they could possibly ever want while others on the planet die of starvation? This seems like a judgment, but to me, it is more about having an understanding about why certain things happen and how this can be changed for the betterment of all humans on this planet.

I think it would be better to encourage people to do good things for each other and to care for one another. Maybe we could be like good parents trying to disempower bad behavior by focusing on what the child does right and to encourage more positive actions, behavior and thoughts and not to just focus on what they are doing wrong. You get more of what you focus on, whatever it is.

59

I encourage you to observe your wrong and right beliefs/stories, to inquire into what lies behind them and ask yourself what it would be like to live beyond the duality of these two sides, seeing mankind as a whole not as wrong and right. Break free from a dualistic viewpoint by having understanding, not judgment.

Chapter 10

Change Your Focus And It Will Enable You To See Deception More Clearly

How do you break free from your limiting belief and stories? Recognizing that they are just stories is the first step. Ultimately somebody made a story up and you believed it, and then owned it like it was your truth. One of the ways I use to recognize stories that I was emotionally invested in was by changing what I was focusing on and by looking at the big picture. Here is an example of what I mean.

Let's use the term "free-range eggs." This marketing term is positioned to stimulate your mind to think that the chickens that lay these eggs are roaming free outside in pastures or paddocks, eating grass, getting exercise, sunshine, and plenty of rest. Well, that's how I used to think of it anyway. I thought that they were cared for, not like other chickens that are housed inside all day and night in the battery chicken farms. So I asked myself, is this view/belief true? Is that what happens to these free-range chickens? I went out to find the real truth. What I found out was that free-range chickens still get fed the same fast growth chemical formulas and laying agents that the battery farms chickens do. I also discovered that the chickens are only allowed to sleep for four hours per night in order to increase egg production. A combination of the laying agents and chemicals they ingest, along with limited sleeping hours, results in the chickens laying two to three eggs per day, a significant increase from the one egg that chickens lay in a natural environment. By the time the free-range hens are a year-and-a-half, they are burnt out and they stop laying eggs. Then they are killed and crushed up into feed for the new chickens.

I questioned my belief story, and I was able to find the real truth. I believe if you change your focus, it can and will change your awareness. Ask questions about your beliefs and you may unlock the truth. You may see what's really going on behind the scenes and start to question where your beliefs have come from. There are lots of very clever deceptions in the world, and if you look behind the words, there might be a completely different story. Here are a couple of my favorites.

The first one is the travel insurance story. Part of the travel insurance charge is in case your luggage gets lost. You pay an airline a lot of money to transport you and your bags to a destination, but if they happen to lose your bags, it's not their fault. So they advise you to pay extra money for flight insurance, as they are so inefficient, they might lose your bags. It would be like going to a dentist and paying an extra $100 insurance in case he or she accidentally pulls out the wrong tooth! Or surgery insurance in case a surgeon replaces the wrong hip (oops, I think someone has already done that). They might have got the big "Sorry about that; we will do the right one for free." And my favorite: the water bottle story. Why is water in plastic water bottles more expensive per liter than petrol in some countries in the world when the water falls out of the sky and is completely free?

How do we see past all of these shrewd illusions into what is really going on? Have our minds been manipulated and marketed to so much that we can only see the world in a certain way? Some companies pay huge amounts of money on advertising campaigns to lure us into thinking that we really need their products or services, and if we buy or use their products, we will be happy and feel successful, liked, and content. Well, maybe not content, because if you were truly content, they wouldn't be able to sell you anything, as you wouldn't need anything. I think that the advertising and marketing people have become the masters of deception, continually and successfully manipulating the thoughts and minds of the masses.

With the fashion industry, young women are strongly targeted with regard to their appearance and self-worth. This focus on appearance seems to last a lifetime for some. I saw a woman about 85 to 90 years old "dressed to the nines." She took great care in presenting herself. It was obvious that her appearance and her image were still very important, possibly so that she would be recognized, admired, seen and accepted. An example of such a person is Queen Elizabeth II. I'm not saying that dressing up isn't fantastic; I feel it is important to take care of our personal appearance for our own sake and our own self-worth. I do, however, at times question the motives of some people in the way they present themselves. What are the stories that drive this? Is it because women love clothes, color, and fashion, or is it that they want to be seen, appreciated, and noticed by others?

Another example of marketing is by Samsung and Apple. They already know what phones they are going to release in two years time as well. Does this make you feel manipulated and controlled?

It sure does to me.

I have used these stories only as an example of the many, many stories there are and the ways that we can be deceived into believing that the world is a certain way. I want to challenge these stories and the validity and truthfulness of them. So how can we see past the illusion, and what tools do we have at our disposal?

A key to see past it is to change your focus, as discussed early in this chapter. Focus on something else besides what you don't have. Focus on being grateful for what you already have. An easy way to seek the truth is to focus on something that is already true, like nature. Choose to focus on plants and flowers, animals, trees, rivers, seas, mountains, and see the reality and the truth that nature already is. See nature with its natural beauty, colors, fragrances, shapes, patterns, movement, rain, wind, clouds, streams, and rivers. True beauty is present in all of this. This primal beauty with its ever-changing landscapes, ever-changing seasons, and ever-changing creations are complex. Be fascinated by the diversity of nature. Be curious that mankind has no control over nature. It keeps changing, moving, growing, circulating, multiplying, thriving, and surviving with very little involvement by man. If anything, mankind is the only thing that upsets the balance in nature. So then, how can humans get back into balance with nature? The natural environment, animals, and wildlife survive without designer jeans, restaurants, insurance, and money. When I get to a place where I find myself wanting this and wanting that, I pause, take a breath, and I go back into nature to think about all that I already have. The need for unnecessary things melts away when I do this.

If I want to change the way I am viewing the world and the deception that seems to be portrayed, I also shift my focus to the poor and needy, the homeless and the starving, the so-called "have not's," and I wonder: how do they survive? I watch documentaries about the lives of people who are struggling on a day-to-day level, and I am constantly amazed by how people survive in appalling conditions with very little food, clean water, and medical attention. I marvel at their ingenuity and their willpower to survive. I watch in awe as they work together in their villages, supporting and helping one another the best they can. Then I bring the focus back to myself and realize I have very little to complain about, if anything at all. It makes me feel that I want to help other people, to give service or assistance to others who are in need and who are not as fortunate as myself. When I think of how I can help others and I focus on other's needs, it gets me out of my stories very quickly and puts things back into perspective.

On a personal level, another way I get out of the deception of my stories is that I practice meditation. This will often bring me to a place of stillness and to my truth of who I really am. Another way that I like to connect is through practicing Qigong and Taiji. They bring me back into a connection with myself through my physical body and help me to connect with the energy inside and outside of myself.

There are a variety of spiritual practices that can bring you to truth and presence, many having philosophies which contribute to the wellbeing of mankind. These philosophies enable you to focus on others and not the stories in your head. Yoga is another very popular and important physical and spiritual practice, which guides you to be in connection with yourself, your physical body, your prana (vital life force), your breath, your mind, and the energy around you, as in many physical energetic practices. Some of these practices use the principle of focusing on others and not on yourself, which I believe is also very helpful to get you out of your head and your stories.

Whatever your practice is, whether it's focusing on helping other people, meditation, Qigong, Taiji, Yoga, walking in nature, or prayer, all of these practices seem to help you to see yourself and the world in a way of connectedness to something larger than yourself. Pick a practice that takes you out of your mind, do it regularly, and you will experience life beyond the deception of your stories and the world.

Exercise 9.

Write your answers in your *Breaking Free* journal.

Title your new page: "How To Change Your Focus And Become More Aware."

We will look at some of the stories that may be stopping you from seeing the bigger picture.

1. What is your bigger picture of partnership and relationships? What do you think relationships are for besides being loved?

2. What is the bigger picture in relation to your occupation? What is your occupation for besides making money?

3. What is the bigger picture in relation to your life? Why are you really here?

4. What stories are true that the media tells you?

   a. Read or watch three pieces of media.
   b. What are they saying?
   c. What do they really want you to think?
   d. What is really the truth?
   e. Who is it targeted to?

5. What stories are advertisers telling you that are true?

   f. Pick three advertisements.
   g. What is the ad selling?
   h. What are they really saying?
   i. Who is it targeted to?
   j. Do you really need it to be happy?

Summary

Change your focus, and it will change your awareness and your perception of the world. If you change the perception of yourself and everybody else in the world by changing your focus, you will be able to see the truth behind the stories, and you will see who you really are and what is really important to you. In return, you will have an extraordinary quality of life. Fuller, richer, and more expansive than you ever thought possible. You will also have more clarity, space, and wisdom. You will have a view outside of yourselves, your opinions and your stories that may be limiting and controlling you. You may see another world outside of your current world, a world that has been hidden by your stories, viewpoints, opinions, and confining beliefs. A world of vastness, excitement, adventure beyond belief. A world of unbound freedom.

Chapter 11

I Can Prove My Story Is True

I have been talking about our stories, the stories that drive and control our lives. To give you a bit more clarity as to what I'm referring to, I will go into some of the stories that have driven me in my life. I personally have lots of stories, like the story, "If I am successful, it will make me a better man" or "If I'm a good father, people will look up to me," and "If I'm a good, honest and a loyal friend, people will respect me." Notice that all these things require me to do something in order to get people to respect and like me so I can feel good about myself. I am sure that my true goal in life is not to get people to like me, but my stories have me believing otherwise. How do we try to prove if our stories are true or false? I am going to use an example, which is not one of mine. (I have lots, but this is not one of them).

This story is called, "Nobody is ever there for me, and I can't trust anybody," which is sort of two stories interrelated to one other. Sometimes if you have one story, you may have the other, but for the purpose of this example, we will say they are just one story. This story can start in many different ways. People who have been adopted may experience this story. The adopted story could be, "My parents didn't want me," or "You can't trust people; even my parents don't want me," or "My parents weren't there for me." Another way this story could have started may have been when your parents broke up, and you didn't see one of them very much anymore. The story could be, "How come I don't hear from my other parent; they're not there for me. I can't trust them." Or you may have had a parent die when you were young, and the story could be, "They were not there for me; I can't trust anybody. If you love someone, they will leave you." These are all valid stories; however, if we remember: these stories were often formulated in the mind of a child, and they don't have the discernment of an adult who has the mental facility to determine whether there is truth to the story. In the mind of a child, the way they saw it was that someone they loved was taken away from them. The "They were not there for me" story forms, or "Because the people who were meant to love and care for me are gone, I can't trust anybody" story can raise its head. These are only some of the origins of the "Nobody is there for me; I can't trust anybody" story; you could imagine the many ways for this story to come into being.

We progress through our lives with these stories running in the background, and then the universe conspires to have events occur that reinforce and fortify these stories. For the "They are not there for me" story, events happen such as, "My father didn't turn up to my school play," or "My mother didn't come to see my first netball or rugby game," or "I wanted to go somewhere but my parents took my brothers and sisters and left me behind at my grandmother's," or "My brother [or sister] was the golden child in the family; they were good at sports and won races; they won all the school awards and got all mum and dad's attention." Or, perhaps, your parents forgot to pick you up from school or that birthday party you missed and you felt they had forgotten you or that you got "left at home alone a lot." Or if one of your parents got a new partner and they spent more time with them than you, or a new baby brother or sister came along and they got all the attention. You can see how the underlying story keeps getting reinforced. It doesn't have to be reinforced every week - just once in a while is enough to keep the story alive. This feeling of rejection and aloneness can stay with you your whole life, from your middle-aged children not spending time with you to your old friends forgetting your birthday.

We can move into relationships with these stories alive and well. Take the story of "Nobody is ever there for me; I can't trust anybody," for example. Sometimes we pick a partner that aligns to and plays out this very underlying story. We pick a partner that stays out, likes to spend time with friends, and withdraws if you try to talk to them. A partner who is not there when you need them both emotionally and physically. A partner who leaves. We can pick partners who have affairs, partners who are disloyal, partners who don't tell the truth, who you don't trust, who run from conflict, and every time they do this, it just proves your story is right, that they are "not there" for you and that you "can't trust anybody." When they leave you, you can say, "See, I told you: nobody is here for me, and I can't trust anybody." So you go to your friends for comfort and support, and they are busy with their own lives and turmoil and aren't there for you either. (I'm not saying that all your friends will not be there for you when you need them, because there will be friends who definitely will; we all generally have friends like this, and we know who they are.)

The "Nobody is here for me" story can be fueled and consolidated many times during one's life. This story quite often influences actions involving people and relationships. Now there is another bizarre twist to how this story can happen. It is what I call "The

Push of Heaven's Finger Phenomenon," which is when some strange force decides to take action and interfere with our story and introduces us to the opposite of our story. In this case, with the "Nobody is there for me" story, you meet a stable, trustworthy, honest, loyal partner who doesn't run, but stands up and supports you. Oh, no! This person doesn't fit your story! What are you going to do? You would think this would be a good thing to help break the story, but not necessarily so. This next response demonstrates just how strong the story can be.

We unconsciously start looking for the faults in this seeming saint of a partner. We don't notice what is right with this person, as that doesn't fit our story. There must be something wrong with them, we decide. We start pushing them away and looking for a sign that they will leave. And when they don't leave, we are not happy, as this doesn't match our story. So then we unconsciously start on a new line of attack by doing out-of-character things just to watch their reaction. We grow angry. We get argumentative. We become unreasonable and loud. We withdraw, looking for the sign. We get totally out of control and then yes, finally, they can't take it anymore, and they leave. Again, we say to ourselves, "See, I told you they're not there for me and that I couldn't trust them." They leave, and our story is still true. We win, sort of, if you call this winning. If you haven't done this yourself, I bet you know somebody who has.

How do we break this destructive story? Recognizing the story is always an important first step. Realize it started as a childhood story, acknowledge that you are no longer a child and that this story doesn't serve you, and come back to the truth - the truth that you are a mature, wise adult living in the present, right here, right now. Your life's happiness is not determined by having somebody there for you or not, and it was never someone else's responsibility to keep you happy. It's yours.

This is only one of the ways we can deal with all the underlying stories like this. I believe the hard part is that we don't necessarily know what stories we have running in the background. If you are brave, you could ask your friends or family you trust or your partner. They will certainly know what some of them are, and funnily enough, their own stories may be tangled up with yours. Why do you think they picked you in the first place? I believe that sometimes we are attracted to people because they are mirrors of our stories and they play out the other side of our story.

Everybody we meet and anyone we have a reaction to is useful in uncovering our underlying stories. So next time you react to someone or a situation, stop and ask yourself, "Why am I reacting to this person or this situation?" This is an incredible tool to help you to become aware and free of the stories that limit you.

Exercise 10.

Write your answers in your *Breaking Free* journal.

Title your new page: "How To Discover My Stories."

> 1. Think of somebody who annoys or upsets you. Write down how they annoy you.

a. What beliefs do I have about this person?

b. Ask yourself, is this really true?

c. Do you have any proof that this is true?

d. Why am I reacting to this person?

e. What do I think they are doing?

f. What do they really want?

g. How could I react differently?

h. Imagine what it would be like not to react to this person.

i. Can you recall an earlier time in your life with another person where this same reaction happened?

2. Think of a situation that annoys or upset you? Write it down.

a. Ask yourself, why am I reacting to this situation?

b. What beliefs do you have about how you think it should be?

c. Are your beliefs true?

d. Do you have any proof that it is true?

e. Imagine what it would be like not to react to this situation.

f. Can you recall an earlier time in your life when this situation or a similar situation happened?

Chapter 12

Understanding Both Sides Of Our Emotions

There are two sides to everything - this is the Yin Yang theory. If happiness is on one side then sadness is on the other. One balances the other out. To experience great happiness, then you may need to experience great sadness, as one is measured against the other. It's like the emotional levels test, where you write down how happy you are on a scale from one to ten, ten being ecstatic, one being depressed. They exist because of their opposites. A matchbox is small compared to a car, but a car is small compared to a bus, and a bus is small compared to an ocean liner. They are all relative to each other. So you can only know happiness compared to sadness. How could you truly understand happiness if you don't have any term of reference to compare it to? Happy, happier, happiest - compared to what? I am happier today than I was yesterday. This I believe is why the psychologists created the scale from one to ten so they would have some way of measuring and calibrating it. But this scale still relies on the two ends of the spectrum, the two polar opposites and the Yin Yang concept.

The strange part about emotions is that we don't seem to experience one without the other. It is unrealistic to feel happy all the time. If you don't want to feel sad, then you may not be able to feel happy either. So not wanting to feel sad may keep you away from experiencing true joy and happiness. If you have a deep desire to feel and experience love, then the fear of feeling unloved might keep you away from it. Now for the catch-22: feeling loved or feeling unloved, I believe, isn't the goal anyway. It's about feeling both feelings together and experiencing what happens when they both come together and create a new field - something that is made up equally of both. It's the Yin and Yang theory. Using the example of respiration, the "in" breath and the "out" breath are Yin and Yang sides that make up the whole breath. Which is more important? If you only have the "in" breath, there is death, and if you only have the other, there is death. It's the two together that create the whole. And in this case, they create life.

You can't separate one side of the coin from the other. It's impossible. You have to have something on the other side of the head. But we try to separate our emotional feelings; we try to separate love and unloved, happiness and sadness. Yet one can't live without the other because of the Universal Law of Yin and Yang. So if you only want to focus on the head side of the coin, you will never see the whole coin, and you will never have any money, literally. The more you focus on wanting to be rich, the more you bring not wanting to be poor into play, and you may find yourself always wanting to be rich and not actually being rich.

So the truth about feeling love or unloved, or happiness and sadness, is to discover what they are a part of. What is the whole coin? To do this you may have to experience both sides equally and not see one as right or wrong. The fear of feeling the sadness and grief if something or someone you love is taken away stops most people from ever seeing the whole coin or fully experiencing love. It is hidden by fear, but unfortunately, it stops you feeling the happiness too.

All you have to do is change the story that you have around feeling unloved and sadness and see them as an experience - not a bad or good experience, just an experience. We have been told that they are bad feelings, but they are not; they are just feelings. If we have made these feelings out to be bad, then we can unmake them. Understanding and feeling our emotions can open a doorway into something truly exciting and liberating. Experience your emotions without judgment or fear. You may need a jackhammer to open them up as these stories of what a bad emotional feeling is could be set in concrete, and the fear and misperceptions could be keeping you away from something extraordinary.

Exercise 11.

Write your answers in your *Breaking Free* journal.

Title a new page: "All Emotions And Feelings Are Useful And Important"

1. On a scale of 1 to 10, 10 being "ecstatic" and 1 being "depressed," where are you right now?

2. Do you think happiness is better than sadness? If so, why?

3. Could your belief stories about happiness and sadness be untrue, and could there be a different way of seeing them?

4. What are happiness and sadness a part of for you? What are they the two sides of?

5. Imagine a life where happiness and sadness are just two different feelings. One is not good and one is not bad. Knowing that there are no right or wrong emotions, that they are all just different, how much more freedom would you experience?

Summary

In Traditional Chinese Medicine (TCM), there is no difference between emotions. They are energies, which are associated with the various organs and meridians. These emotions have a healthy flow and are used to diagnose conditions when the emotions are out of balance. It's not whether they are sad, as it is normal to sometimes experience sadness; however, if an individual is sad all the time, then this is an imbalance in their body's energy, which in this case directly affects the Lung Meridian.

When does this separation of identifying emotions as "good" or "bad" start? I believe very early in most cases. For example, when a mother tries to "fix" her crying child by saying, "Come over here, and I will make you feel better," what she is unconsciously saying is that feeling sadness is not good, and you need to fix it or make it better. And this is how the separation of Yin and Yang emotions starts, and it can start as early as when we are infants. An alternative could be to pick up the child and say, "Have a good cry; it's good for you, and I love you," or if they are angry, give them a pillow and tell them to bang it against the floor to allow them to release the anger energy in a constructive way. Maybe if we were all encouraged at an early age to see emotions differently, we might not spend the rest of our lives trying to avoid feeling emotions that we believe are wrong or negative.

See if you can view your emotions in a new way, enabling you to see a bigger picture and ultimately gain more understanding and freedom. Feeling all emotions is normal and none are wrong or right. They are different feelings and experiences we have as humans.

Different Belief Stories

Chapter 13

How To Unlock The Truth About Your Stories

How do we recognize the stories for what they really are - just stories? I discovered that I have defined myself by my stories. I had based my opinions and beliefs about life from believing in these stories. So I set about deconstructing some of the stories that had control over me. One of the things I discovered is that I had a lot of judgment if someone didn't agree with me - an example of the "I'm right, you're wrong" story. I had a story about money and prosperity that said, "I always have to struggle, and life is always going to be difficult." To find the origins and accuracy of these stories, I started asking people I trust about the truthfulness of my stories. Soon I discovered that if they had the same stories, they would agree with me, which didn't help my prognosis! I decided to start looking into a story that I was told by my parents. The story was, "If you win the Lotto (Lottery), you will be happy." The truth of this story crashed straight away when I saw people on TV who had won the Lotto and even they still had not achieved true happiness. I've also seen people without money that were not happy, and I have seen both rich and poor people who are happy.

So I came to the conclusion that money is not the key to happiness.

The Lotto advertisements always show happy, smiling people jumping up in the air with joy. They show people who, after winning the Lotto, have all the things they ever wanted. So I asked myself, what is the "Money makes you happy" story? I realized the goal of this story is to feel happy. It wasn't about the money even though it appeared to be. I asked myself: *Is money the only thing that makes me happy? What else makes me happy? My daughter, my son, my partner, my friends, material things, experiences in my life, my work, hobbies?* When I realized the story was actually all about just being happy and not about what makes me happy, I asked myself the next question: *Is happiness the goal in life?*

First of all, I needed to understand what happiness really was. Was it a feeling, a state of mind, a state of wellbeing? Then I realized the story was about just wanting to be happy. Now, if my goal is to be happy all the time, then I'm doomed for failure right from the start. How could I possibly be happy all the time? That's pretty much impossible because sometimes I might get angry if somebody stands on my toes or I will be sad if somebody I know dies. I also know that if I create happy emotions, then I create unhappy emotions too, as goes the Yin Yang principle. The polar opposite has to exist; it is the Law of Polarity clearly evident in nature through the north and south poles. My next question was: *What are the two sides of happy and sad?* The Yin and Yang theory determines they are just two sides of a whole. So what is the whole that they are a part of? What is in the middle? Where are they joined? Maybe the whole is that they are just emotions and one day I might feel happy and another day I might feel sad. One minute I might feel one emotion and another minute I might feel something different. Maybe the key is to come to a place of acceptance of what is? Then the next obvious question popped up: *What are emotions?* I know that there is no point chasing happiness because I know I will feel it at some time, as I will feel all emotions at some time.

Now let's go back to the Lotto story. Do I need money to make me happy? No, I can choose to be happy at any time. I also know that I will feel happy sometimes anyway. Having money isn't about feeling happy - that's not true. Happiness is a choice as is any emotion, even though it may not seem to be at the time. What is money then? You can see the inquiry into the origin of my stories just goes deeper and deeper. Remember they are just stories, and if we can see past their illusion, they are not good or bad, they just are, and by accepting them as they are, without opinions, they have no power.

I hope that, whatever emotion you are feeling - happy, sad, confused, and so on - you know that the feeling is okay. I know you will be feeling something. Even "blank" is something. I am now free from the "Money makes you happy" story and maybe you are too. I bet some of you still think money will make you happy and that's okay, as these stories have been embedded in our psyches for a long time and may not go away after reading a few words. I've planted an idea, a seed in your mind now, and it's going to challenge your current belief structures. Careful - you may start questioning some of your other beliefs and their validity. Then you may become free from them, whatever free is, and that may be another story.

Exercise 12.

Write your answers in your *Breaking Free* journal.

Title your new page: "What Really Makes Me Happy."

1. Write a list and start with:

   If I had _____, I would be happy because _____.

   For example: If I had a house, I would be happy because I would feel I had financial security.

2. After you write your list, go back to each point and ask yourself, "Is it true?" Then ask yourself, "What proof do I have that it is true?" and "What proof do I have that it is absolutely true?"

Summary

Questioning our beliefs around money and discovering the stories we have around wealth and finance is a great way to uncover some of our underlying stories. If we have stories about money, then we might have stories about a lot of other things in our lives as well. Questioning our reality is a powerful way to free ourselves from our underlying stories that are limiting us.

Chapter 14

When They Win, I'm Happy

I have noticed a strange behavior and fixation among the human race: an obsession with watching our favorite sports teams and with winning. Why is it that I'm happy when my sports team wins, and I'm unhappy when they lose? How is it that I can base some of my emotional happiness on whether or not the New Zealand All Blacks rugby team wins? Watching and participating in sports has a huge following worldwide, from chess to arm wrestling to the Super Bowl, Olympics, and so on. We seem to compete in every sport imaginable in every age group, males and females, in every country, in the air, on land, and in the water. There are obscure sports like giant pumpkin kayaking and bog snorkeling, which seems to be about winning and being better at something than somebody else. (Or maybe it's about just having fun?)

Why does it feel so good to win and feel so bad to lose? Why does losing create a feeling of emptiness, or sadness, and in some cases I have observed, even despair? In New Zealand where I'm from, when the All Blacks rugby team loses, I have witnessed people getting outright angry. I wonder what is this addiction to winning? Obviously, it makes some of us feel good to win, but why? What is this built-in competitiveness we have as humans? It may have started as a survival instinct to compete for food, water or land, or mates. (Funnily enough, the latter one still happens today.) Or is it even more primal than that regarding the will to survive, and/or survival of the fittest?

In our modern age, I think competitiveness starts at an early age with comments from our parents like, "I bet I can run faster than you," and "Ha, I beat you," or "I bet even your sister could beat you," or "Your brother isn't as messy as you," or "You better run fast or your uncle Harry will catch you." Then you go to school, where they play games, and when you get home, you tell your dad you had a race and his first comment may be, "Did you win?" or "What place did you come in?" In the classroom, you have tests and the kids know who got the highest marks and who got the lowest. The child who got the highest mark always feels better than the child who got the lowest.

In playing sports, any sport, we are set up to believe that the ultimate goal is to win. Some people do play sports for the fun of it, but generally, it's about winning. To me, losing is still not much fun, which is not surprising as I was brought up by two competitive sports-playing parents. So you can see why I might be just a little bit competitive. I also appreciate that some people don't mind losing, but in my observations, that is not the norm. Why does it feel good to be better at something than somebody else? Of course, this is not everybody's story. This addiction to the feeling of winning doesn't seem to stop when we stop playing sports either. It's in business, politics, and religion. It is between states, provinces, and countries. When people stop playing sports, they can adopt a team or sports star to follow and then they are happy when they win. What is this strange phenomenon that drives society? What is this need to be better than somebody else to make us feel happy or content or fulfilled? I know there is a reward in pushing yourself to excel and to push yourself to a higher level of endurance and success. I'm not talking about that part. I'm talking about the emotional attachment to winning and losing.

I ask myself why I want to be better than somebody else. Why, in my psyche, does that make me experience a feeling of elation? How can I give my choice to be happy away to a bunch of rugby players who I don't even know? It's a weird thing, this competitive thing. It's like wanting to get the car parked before the other person, or getting to the checkout counter quicker than somebody else in another lane or not letting somebody into the queue of cars. Maybe it does stem back to wars with swords and spears. If you weren't skilled and competitive, you died. Watch the All Blacks play. Is it, once again, the primal urge to survive? The warrior mindset: strength against strength, skill against skill?

I think the ironic part to this story is: How can we compare ourselves with other humans when our makeup is completely different to theirs? There are no two people ever born the same or ever will be. DNA has proven that. It's like comparing apples with lemons. They are both very different, but they are still fruits. I understand the principle that we are all unique and it's only a game, but I still go and watch the All Blacks play. Maybe that's what I and millions of other people like, these sometimes termed "gladiator sports." Maybe it's because it's illegal to go out and fight with people or beat them and take their house and land. (In many countries, this still happens.) It seems that some countries have real wars and other countries just play games of sport to see who is the best. Some countries even manage to have fights and sport at the same time like in English football. I wonder why we still need to vent this part of our instinct even after we have become a so-called civilized culture? Maybe we can't ignore our instinct to survive and our competitiveness, but we can redirect it to be a less harmful way of expressing it.

There are great lessons to be learned from losing. The question here should be "What are you really losing anyway?" Your pride, your dignity, your self-esteem? Or has it got nothing to do with these at all? Maybe it could be seen as a great opportunity to improve? I remember saying to my son when he lost in a game of hockey, "So what did you do well at, and what could you do to improve your game and your skills?" And then I said, "What did the team do well at, and what could they improve on?" Losing has a major positive element that winning does not have. Losing allows you to see what the winning team did better than you did, so you have a focus on what to improve upon. If you win all the time, what do you do to improve? I believe this is why it is so hard to stay at the top of any sport; by winning, in a weird way, you are helping your opposition become better than you.

A great example of this would be the 2013 America's Cup Yachting Final where the New Zealand team was up eight races to nil over Oracle Team USA. One of the skills that the New Zealand team had learned to do was to tack from one side to the other without coming down off the dagger boards and foils, which allows the yachts to hydrofoil at up to 50 knots. The Americans observed this, and then they started practicing how to do it themselves. With a few design changes, an already faster yacht, watching carefully, and replicating the sailing techniques of the New Zealand team, they went on to win the next nine races in a row and then to win the Americas Cup. It's one of the great comeback stories motivated by the drive to be the best in the world. They observed what their opponents were doing more efficiently than them, learned from it, adapted, and then became victorious.

Exercise 13.

Write your answers in your *Breaking Free* journal.

Title your new page: "I Compete To Grow Myself."

1. Write a list of some of the ways that you are competitive. For example: at work, driving a car, in sports, with your children.

2. How do you feel if you win?

3. How do you feel if you lose?

4. Why do you think that winning is important?

5. What do you think happens when you lose?

6. Do you think your answers are true?

7. Go back to questions 2 to 5, and ask yourself the same questions again. Go deeper now that you have had time to think about.

Chapter 15

Is The Goal Of Money To Bring You Happiness?

I was talking to a friend the other day at breakfast, and he commented that I was talking a lot about money and how I seemed to have an attachment to achieving financial security. He started a line of questioning with me around why I wanted to achieve financial security. Through this line of questioning, we discovered that my key driving force was primarily based around wanting the freedom to travel - to do whatever I wanted and not have to worry about working and paying bills. He asked me why I really wanted to travel; what was I going to get out of travel? I said that it would make me happy. Then it hit me. I was giving my power away to money. I made the assumption that not only would it make me happy, but also that this happiness was way off in the future because I had to generate lots of money before I would have enough to travel the world and achieve this so-called financial security.

I had fallen into the trap again: the trap of believing that something outside of myself was going to result in my happiness. I had made the same mistake previously, where I so desperately wanted people to like me that I handed over my personal power. If they accepted and liked me, I was okay. Through my friend's questioning, I was able to witness myself looking for external circumstances to create happiness again, this time with money.

It is so easy to attach happiness to something outside of us and to then project this happiness into the future. I believe the key to contentment is to have gratitude for what you have right now in your life and acknowledge all the gifts - from your friends to your car, your home, and job. By having gratitude for what we have in the present moment, we attract more of the same. If you are in a situation that you are not currently happy with, it is okay to acknowledge your unhappiness. You can then be grateful that you have the power to change the circumstance, should you wish. No matter how grim the situation may seem, and even if you feel like you have no choice, it's not true; you always have a choice. Even if you don't want to make that particular decision, you still have a choice.

Now that I have taken my happiness away from the future, away from travel, and brought it back home - to right here, right now - it has made my life a lot easier, fuller, and I am more content. I still want to travel, but I am now happy in the process of manifesting the experience, happy saving for it, happy planning for it, and knowing that I will have this experience soon.

Exercise 14.

Write your answers in your *Breaking Free* journal.

Title your new page: "I Choose To Be Happy Right Now."

1. Write a list of the things that make you happy.
2. Is something stopping you from being happy right now?
3. What changes could you make right now to make your life more positive?

Chapter 16

You Make Me Angry

How can anybody make me angry? I believe that no one can make me feel angry; however, my reaction towards a person may be expressed in anger. Nobody can make me do anything or feel anything. Ultimately it is my choice as to how I respond to certain people, situations, or circumstances.

If we go even deeper, we can start to examine where anger actually comes from.

There is a common understanding that anger comes from getting one or several of our goals blocked by an external source. Check this theory out for yourself. Think of a time or an event when you got angry. What was your goal? What were you trying to achieve, and how was it being stopped? What were you trying to achieve with your goal in the first place? Was it something to make you feel happy or successful or to look good, be appreciated, valued, heard, or loved? You know what is coming next, don't you? Yes, the next level down. Why do you want to feel happy or successful, appreciated, valued, heard, or loved? And yes, the next level down: why don't you feel these things already? If we go down another level still: why do you think that it is important to experience feelings of success and appreciation and being valued, heard, and loved in the first place? If you don't feel that these goals are being met at the time, it is possible that you may experience anger.

What if the goal was to live in the present and acknowledge that whatever you are feeling is okay, whether you feel happy, angry, sad, heard or not heard, valued or not valued, loved or not loved? Maybe it's all okay. All feelings are okay. By having no attachment to them, they are what they are. None are good or bad. They are emotions that create different experiences. Maybe if we could just see them as experiences of life and not good or bad, we would experience life a different way, one without failure or judgment, one with understanding and gratitude, one with openness, clarity, and freedom. Wouldn't that be great? I could feel angry and not blame anybody else including myself. Wouldn't that be an interesting and empowering feeling?

Exercise 15.

Write your answers in your *Breaking Free* journal.

Title a new page: "Nothing Can Make Me Angry."

    1. Write a list of the things that make you angry.

        For example:
        a. Waiting a long time at a restaurant for your meal.
        b. People pulling out in front of you without looking while driving.
        c. When you think you give good advice and people don't listen.

    2. What were the goals that you wanted to achieve for each of your examples?

3. Often we get angry because our goals have been blocked. Now you have discovered what your goals are, ask yourself, what beliefs are driving each of your goals, and are these beliefs about what you think you should achieve in life really true?

Summary

When you have an emotional "charge" about something, it is useful to inquire into the underlying story that may be driving it. What causes the anger? What goal is being blocked? What drives your worry; what are you really worried about? To be free from our stories, we may need to discover what the underlying belief is and accept that it may not be true.

Chapter 17

The Power In Taking Responsibility
For Your Actions

This is easy to say, but not necessarily easy to do. What I do know is that there is a freedom that comes with taking full responsibility for your actions, which I have personally found to be very rewarding. I used to say a lot, and at times still catch myself saying things like, "It's their fault," or "She made me feel like this," or "If it wasn't for him, I wouldn't have done X," or "What about your part in it?" or "I wouldn't have done it if it wasn't for you." It's a basic human protection mechanism to not want to be wrong, or do something that could be perceived as wrong. In the instance that something is actually wrong, then something must be right, right? Whose set of moral rules did the wrong and right judgments actually come from? From our parents, school, society, religious belief, or maybe just a personal belief? I believe the "wrong" and "right" rules that we have come from our own values, but then the question is: Where did you get your values? We know for sure that everybody has their own set of values and we also know these values differ largely from person to person, family to family, and country to country. But whose sets of values are right? Of course I think my set of values are right; you may think your values are right too, but we may want to check where we got them from and whether they actually are true.

I believe the truth is that we do make mistakes, and we can say inappropriate or non-compassionate things at times. But maybe we are a little hard on ourselves. We are not perfect and never can be and neither can anybody else be. I have gone through the "trying to be a perfect" phase of my life. This behavior can be driven by many things. My story was, "If I am perfect, I won't make any mistakes, and then people will like and respect me." I have discovered that this is not true at all. When I made a mistake (and I always will especially while I have a set of rules about wrong and right), I always had to find something or someone else to blame for what happened. It was always someone else's fault. If I took responsibility that it was my fault, then I had failed, and the feeling of being useless and hopeless came flooding back. These feelings were like death to me, so I would do anything to avoid them. What a huge responsibility to put on myself. Constantly trying to never make a mistake is stressful.

The truth is that we are perfect. Perfect in our humanness and imperfection, and that we all make mistakes. Isn't it that when we make mistakes, we can have our biggest growth? In theory, we should be encouraging mistakes so we can keep learning, evolving, and growing. The freedom from accepting this is amazing. This has been another step for me towards becoming free from my limiting belief stories. Now I try to be responsible for my actions all the time. Notice I mentioned the word "try."

I think the more we step into taking responsibility for our actions and mistakes, the more we give other people the permission to do this too. It takes bravery and courage to stand up and let people see you as you are, the real you. Be the example. Be the inspiration. Encourage others to stand up. It is a powerful thing to do.

Exercise 16.

Write your answers in your *Breaking Free* journal.

Title a new page: "I Take Responsibility For My Actions."

>   1. What do you do if you make a mistake? Do you own it, or try to get out of it by blaming somebody else or by blaming a circumstance? (If you are not sure, ask your partner or your best friend; they will know.)

>   2. After you have discovered how you respond to making a mistake, write down any emotions that arise and the feelings provoked. Stay with the feelings and inquire into any other times you have experienced them.

>   3. Then write down how else you could have responded in a way that would be more empowering for you.

Summary

I believe a true sign of courage and integrity is to own your own humanness and that means owning all of your actions, choices, and decisions.

Chapter 18

Is It Really Betrayal?

In this story, I am going to use the feeling of betrayal as a way to illustrate how we create expectations of others and how this can cause us pain. It is also an example of how we can reinforce our limiting belief stories.

According to Wikipedia, "Betrayal is the breaking or violation of a presumptive contract, trust, or confidence that produces moral and psychological conflict within a relationship amongst individuals, between organizations or between individuals and organizations."

Can anybody really betray you, or do they betray the set of expectations you have set for them to keep? Or is it that they just don't live up to your story of what you think loyalty, honesty, and integrity should be? Have we made up a picture of what we think defines an honest, loyal person, and do we then live up to our own definition of what we think an honest person should be and do? Do we truly want honest people like that around us? Could the truth really be that we just want honest people around us so that we can never feel the feelings that come with betrayal?

Is it a betrayal that we fear or is it the feelings that come with the betrayal that we fear? The feeling of betrayal can bring up feelings of rejection, being alone or abandoned, like you can't trust anybody, or it may be something else entirely. I believe the truth is that it is not the betrayal, but the feelings evoked by the betrayal that we don't want to feel.

How I have prevented this from happening to me in my life is by positioning people around me who I believe are loyal so that I can limit the experience of feeling betrayed, which evokes feelings of rejection, abandonment, or aloneness. I call these people the people of my inner circle, people whom I trust, people who will not let me down, who will be there for me, who will keep me safe. But I have burdened these people with expectations that they should behave in the way I want them to behave so that I can feel safe. Safe from the rejection, abandonment, and loneliness.

I believe it is unfair to expect my friends to maintain the standards I have set for them. The ironic part of this is that they don't even know the standards they're meant to be keeping, as we have never had a conversation about them. To expect my friends to always be there for me no matter what their circumstances are is an unrealistic expectation. I also expect myself to maintain these standards, causing myself unnecessary pressure in the process. To always be loyal to my friends, to always be there for them, and to always be trustworthy and honest is nearly impossible to sustain 100% of the time.

I'm not saying that these aren't good moral standards to adhere to; I'm saying it is difficult to be "perfect" all the time, if possible at all. There is no allowance for humanness, unintentional lapses, or mistakes. Within these rules, there is no room for human error; therefore, there is a high possibility and chance of failure. When I set such high perfect standards, how will I feel if I make a mistake?

Probably the same way I will feel if one of my friends lets me down. I think I have set my friends and myself an impossible goal to achieve and an unrealistic one at that.

I believe I need to accept my friends as they are. If they are loyal, they are loyal to whatever degree that is. If they're not, then they are not, and it's okay either way. Just as with my friends, it is important to remove expectations and accept myself for who I am and what I am capable of at any given moment. By not burdening myself with such rigid rules and unachievable standards, it may also alleviate judgments on how I should or should not behave. This is not to say that I won't always try to maintain a healthy set of standards, but I have more space around them and less judgment, which in turn allows me to have less judgment on others and helps me to appreciate and understand other people's humanness and imperfections.

This also applies to my wife, Josephine. To burden her with a set of expectations that she should always be there for me, never betray me, always be 100% honest with me, perfect, and never making mistakes is an unfair expectation to put on her. I have freed her from this responsibility. I accept her the way she is, and I take away all expectations that she should be anybody other than herself.

I have taken the pressure off myself as well. The pressure to be perfect is an unfair expectation. This is just another step of freeing myself from limiting belief stories that I have been carrying around for most of my life, holding myself ransom to the idea that I have to be a certain way and that's the only way I can be. Having expectations and judgments on the way people should behave according to my set of rules is unrealistic, unfair, and unreasonable.

So now I am loyal to the best of my ability. I am honest the best way I can be, and I show integrity the best way that I can while having no expectation that anybody else should do the same.

Exercise 17.

Write your answers in your *Breaking Free* journal.

Title a new page: "I'm Free From Expectations."

1. Write down any time in your life that you have felt betrayed.

2. Write down the expectations you had with this person or event.

3. Do you have these expectations of yourself as well? Write down the expectation you have for yourself around loyalty and betrayal.

4. What do you feel if your expectations aren't met?

5. How do you react if your expectations aren't met?

6. How would you see yourself if you had no expectations on you, just acceptance?

7. How free does that make you feel?

8. How would you see other people if you had no expectations of them, just acceptance?

Summary

Life is easier for me now that I have removed some of the pressure off of others and myself around expectations. Nobody can ever let me down if I don't have expectations for them to be someone other than who they really are. I accept myself for just who I am, warts and all, not that I have any warts.

Chapter 19

I Don't Like Being Put Down

In this chapter, I explore another example of limiting belief stories and how these stories play out in our lives. What is truly underneath and driving these stories? Are there feelings that we don't want to feel that come with the stories? The example I am going to use is the feeling that comes when I experience being put down.

I don't like being put down, and I don't think that I'm alone in this. This goes right back to my childhood with my parents making statements to me like, "Stop being a show-off," or "Don't be a skite," or "Don't be boastful," or "Who do you think you are?" How disempowering are these statements for a young child to hear? I encouraged my own children to stand up and be their wonderful selves - to be seen, to speak their minds, to have opinions, to ask questions, to discover their true characters and personalities and to question and challenge things told to them. The teachers at school may not have thanked me for that. However, I wasn't encouraged to do that as a child, and I really believe that everyone should have the freedom and confidence to be able to express who they are. In my parents' generation, you weren't allowed to stand up and be seen or heard or to stand up and make a fool of yourself, whatever making a fool of yourself really is. Maybe they were just standing up expressing themselves in their true, glorious warts-and-all self.

I mentioned the tall poppy syndrome earlier. It is a syndrome that condemns people for standing up and being willing to be seen in all their magnificence. What is wrong with people standing in their greatness? I have heard some people say, "Well if people stand up and put themselves on a platform/pedestal, it's because they are arrogant and full of themselves; they will become overpowering, pushy, overly confident and overbearing." I question where these thoughts and beliefs come from. Their parents? Why can't we celebrate greatness and not be threatened by overachievement or whatever the story is we have around excellence and extraordinary people? The USA is very good for praising people for their greatness and celebrating their successes.

So back to my fear of being put down. It's not the fear of being put down that is the problem; it's the feeling of disempowerment that comes with it that I didn't like. This feeling penetrates my whole body. It's combined with feelings of worthlessness, hopelessness, inadequacy, and in my case, a feeling that there is something wrong with me. This story had been driving me for a long time, and it had been the fundamental force behind a lot of the choices I've made.

If you were trying to avoid being put down, what methods would you use? This is what I did. First of all, I decided that I could never make a mistake. I ensured that I knew everything about everything, covering all subjects so nobody could ever fault my comments. I existed in a constant state of having to fix myself so that there was nothing wrong with me. I became a perfectionist, a teacher, and a medical practitioner - a perfectionist so I didn't make mistakes, the teacher because I had to know the truth and all the answers to the questions, and the medical practitioner so I could fix myself and make sure that there was nothing wrong with me. I become the perfect example of health, no drugs, no alcohol, no coffee, no additives, and no preservatives. No one would be able to find any fault in my diet. It would be perfect. I made sure of that. What was fueling this level of perfectionism? It wasn't that I just wanted great health; it was that I didn't want to feel the feeling of being a failure. I've said before, it's not what you do; it's why you do it.

I'm sure you can imagine how hard it was maintaining these rigid constraints in my life. Being a perfectionist is such work. Having to cover all possible eventualities, to cover all bases and protect this image takes consistent supervision and vigilance. Never being able to make a mistake in your life is an absurd burden to have. You will know the people in your life that can't make mistakes: they can never be wrong, it's always somebody else's fault, and they will always have an excuse, but it is coming from a story of lack of self-worth running in the background.

I overcame this first by understanding and realizing that no two people are the same, ever were or ever could be. How can I compare myself to somebody else in that case? Secondly, I came to an awakening that nobody can be perfect; it's impossible. Lastly, I didn't need to fix myself and everybody else; I was already fixed!

What I have learned is that we are already perfect and unique the way we are. We are not broken. We don't need to be fixed. Any belief that you need "fixing" is just a story that would have you believe otherwise. When you are being yourself, others may put you down or seem to be putting you down. It may be coming from their judgment or opinion and there may even be an element of truth in what they say. Either way, it could be a great opportunity

107

to inquire into your reactions and a chance to learn more about yourself. In the end, it is important for you to be okay with who you truly are and not feel the need to defend yourself.

Be free. Be yourself. Be kind to yourself and others. Is there really much else to do?

Exercise 18.

Write your answers in your *Breaking Free* journal.

Title a new page: "I See The Best In People And Only Raise Their Self-Esteem."

1. Who puts you down in your life?

2. How does it make you feel?

3. How do you respond when they do this?

4. What would be a more empowering way to react if somebody did put you down?

5. Do you put people down and why them in particular?

6. How would it feel to never be put down again and to never put down another person?

Summary

I now know that no one can be perfect or ever could be. A teacher doesn't know everything. That is impossible. A medical practitioner gets sick sometimes, too, and they can't fix everyone. The weight that I was carrying from the burden of these old stories was intense. Now I have become freer and lighter, and I can't be put down if I don't have anything to defend.

I know I have more stories running in the background and that's okay. As my friend Ray says, "Hey, you have to have something to do to fill your days." Because I'm not so much of a perfectionist in a destructive way now, I don't have to have all the old stories sorted out at once. I have plenty of time, and you can't put me down for that. I will say, though, that I think having high personal standards is a great thing; I'm just way more flexible around this now, which gives me more freedom.

Now I can just worry about what is really important, such as what am I going to have for dinner. And I'm not too worried about that either.

Chapter 20

Why Do I Need To Be Busy?

I have often wondered why I can't sit still and simply do nothing. I often feel agitated and want to stand up and do something. So I set out to uncover what I was feeling that made me feel so uncomfortable about sitting still.

Sitting in the stillness and quietness, I realized the feeling that I was experiencing in this place was a feeling of loneliness. In this place, I felt solitude. It took me back to memories of my childhood, of being by myself and feeling lonely. It was this feeling I didn't want to feel. How I used to alleviate this feeling was to get busy, fill up the gap and space by doing something to occupy my mind from feeling such deadly silence. Well, it felt like death to me anyway.

I have talked with other people about this, and they have had similar experiences. They all have implemented different ways of filling up their own emptiness and quietness. Some shared ways of keeping their minds busy by watching television, turning on the radio, reading books or doing housework, anything to distract them from the quietness. Some said they couldn't sit still for a time without starting to fidget, and some even found that reading a book created too much quietness for them. I think this phenomenon comes from not really understanding the quietness; maybe this stillness has been misinterpreted. For some people I know, quietness is a place of boredom. Some might feel that they are wasting their time or wasting their life by not being productive. I believe not wanting to experience the feeling that comes with the quietness, stillness or emptiness drives people to do what they do. Keeping the mind busy stops them from feeling the emptiness. Even when people start to meditate, their minds become very busy trying to keep occupied so it doesn't have to enter into this quiet space of stillness.

The ironic part is that when I am by myself practicing Taiji in the morning, I like being in that place of quietness, tranquility, and solitude. It's a place where I feel connected to myself and connected to nature. But if I'm by myself not doing Taiji and it is quiet and peaceful, I see that space as loneliness. It could be that because I'm moving while exercising slowly, it gives my mind and body something to do. It's interesting that I perceive one to be okay and not the other.

I realized that I have been mistakenly seeing the quietness as a bad place to be when in fact it is really somewhere I long to be at the beginning of each day. I wonder if I'm not the only one who does this, who has mistaken quietness and tranquility as a place of being lazy, of wasting my life away, or as being a place of loneliness?

I encourage you to sit in the quietness and watch what stories come up about why it is or isn't a good place to be for you personally. I also know there will be people very comfortable in the space, and they won't have any stories around sitting quietly by themselves.

Work out what feelings come up while you are sitting still. It could be a feeling that sounds like this: *You're lazy. You are wasting your life. You will never accomplish anything in life just sitting around. You are wasting time. You're useless. You are idle. You are wasting your talents. You will never make anything of your life. You will have no friends. Nobody wants to be with you.* The list of stories goes on and on. I believe all these stories lead back to a core story, that you feel you're not good enough or lovable.

But are the stories true? Or are they just a distraction to keep you away from one of the most blissful states of consciousness, a place of stillness, peace, contentment, and tranquility? Monks and nuns have spent 20+ years in caves (retreats, monasteries, convents) to discover this. Maybe we don't have to do that. Maybe we just need to sit and watch the feelings that arise and then notice where we feel that feeling in our bodies. Find what story comes up, ask yourself if that story is true, and then create a more empowering story. You made it up, so I'm sure you can unmake it up. It's just that simple.

The story about sitting alone quietly was triggered by the feeling of loneliness sparked by events that happened in my childhood when I was by myself. The truth is that I know now I can never truly be alone. For a start, I have all the different parts of my personality to keep me company. I have my perception, which is spiritually looking after me, and this huge energy field called mankind, let alone every plant, flower, tree, animal, mountain, river, sea, and cloud and not to mention every star and planet. If anything, it's a bit crowded.

I now look forward to finding some peace and quiet each day of my life. I am comfortable with the quietness and stillness. To just be able to sit with myself and be content, to just be with myself and not need to occupy my mind with activities, is a great step forward in being at peace with myself. I want to have a balance of both, being active and remaining quiet. I think this could take a while to perfect, and it will take practice. I think this is why they call it a "spiritual practice," because it is something that I need to practice daily.

What do you fill your loneliness or emptiness with? Or could you be one of those lucky people who are very comfortable in the silence? There is a lot of space and possibility in the silence for me now, and I acknowledge this place for me is not a place of loneliness but a place of connection and inner peace.

Exercise 19.

Write your answers in your *Breaking Free* journal.

Title a new page: "I Can Never Be Alone."

1. Sit quietly and see what comes up for you. See what emerges by sitting there quietly.

2. Where did the feeling originate from?

3. Are they true, really true?

4. If what you felt was a negative response, see if you can replace it with a different understanding of what being by yourself and sitting quietly really is. Write down what this place of quietness could be for you.

Summary

What has helped me to have a fuller and more abundant life has been changing my mind around how I see things - changing my stories. I now know I am never alone and I now value quietness. I encourage you to open your mind to see new possibilities and a new understanding of the terms "being alone" or "loneliness." Maybe you could change it to "having peace and quiet" and "having your own space."

Chapter 21

What Creates An Overly Busy Mind?

Our mind is an incredible tool. Doctors and scientists have been conducting research on how it works and functions for many years. Even now they have only touched the tip of the iceberg in their research in discovering the complexities and functionality of how our brains and our minds work. There are some very brilliant thinkers in the world that have created mind-blowing breakthroughs in our understanding of human science, biology and quantum physics, human behavior and our physical conditions. There is a downside to our minds' ability to contemplate, wonder, speculate, fathom, ponder, problem-solve, conjecture, ruminate and theorize: we have created a world of overthinking.

I think the mind is one of the most marvelous and complex parts of being human and of our existence. We know it has many functions and is the control center for all activity for the body, from remembering every minute of our lives to keeping our heart beating, our lungs breathing and even by telling us what foods to eat. It is a truly an amazing part of the human body. But as science increases its knowledge of the functionality of the human body, and our understanding of cells, genes, and DNA grows, we have come to realize that our memory is stored in every cell in the body and not just the brain. All that we ever experience and all that we ever know is stored in every single cell, as if a giant wet cell memory card. Our brain is the processor of this information that passes throughout the body. From the interpretation of the five senses and possibly six or seven, it constantly makes decisions and deductions about what is happening around us and is permanently in survival mode. Survival mode does not mean fight and flight mode, but a normal homeostasis self-preservation mode. Not only does it remember everything that happens to you in your life, but it also predicts the future by making moment-by-moment calculations and split-second decisions to keep you well, safe, and alive.

In the physical aspect of the body, the mind center tells the heart to beat faster when we are walking, it tells the body to heat up if it's cold, it tells the body to heal itself if it gets cut, and tells it to start running if there is danger. There are myriads and myriads of other physical functions that the mind controls on a day-to-day basis. The truth is that our own mind can't even fathom or understand how incredible it actually is.

As useful and complex as our minds are, from a spiritual level the mind is sometimes seen as the problem, the very thing that stands in the road of enlightenment, stillness, and tranquility. Our busy minds can be the very thing that can unhinge the most dedicated meditator. In the search for spiritual connection, our busy minds can interfere with this process as we search for a place where our minds are quiet. It is said in some meditation practices that one of the goals is to try to find a gap between two thoughts or the quietness between two breaths where the mind is still and you are *present* without any busy thoughts invading this space. The craziness of this is that your mind is asking your mind to be quiet. Try and get your head around that! Who is talking to whom?

On a medical level, this over-rumination can cause stress, anxiety, worry, and depression. In Traditional Chinese Medicine, this over-pensiveness can and does cause all forms of Qi stagnations, depletions, and disharmonies, and is the cause of many illnesses and sicknesses in the body.

If you think you are in control of what the mind thinks about, then can you make it be quiet and still if you want to at anytime? Who is really in control of your mind? If it isn't you, then who is in charge.

In my understanding of mental mastery, you are in control of what you think, you watch your thoughts come and go, and you choose what to focus on and want to let go of. You have mindfulness around the activity of your thoughts. You have control over your reactions to your thoughts, and you know that you are not your thoughts; you are the observer of your thoughts. I have also experienced a place beyond being the observer where the observer doesn't exist either. To have mental mastery takes practice, but first you need to understand where your thoughts are coming from and what is triggering these thoughts to come into your consciousness.

What the mind does when you are doing something for the first time is try to remember other occasions or events that were similar to what is happening now. It uses these old experiences as a term of reference to try and make some sense of this new situation. It can often totally misconstrue the situation. We give the mind the right to interpret and to intervene in the situation, primarily as one of safety and secondly, unwittingly, we can give it control of a situation that it doesn't necessary need to be in control of. I believe this is the foundation of why our minds seem to have so much control over us. The mind not only wants to keep us physically safe, but emotionally safe too. But safe from what? I believe there are two parts to this: physical safety and secondly, emotional safety. It's the second part that I want to inquire into.

I believe without realizing, we have given our mind control to keep us emotionally safe. Safe from emotional pain and suffering and to help us avoid feelings we don't want to feel. And because subconsciously our minds have been given control over our emotional feelings and because our minds already have control over everything else, it seems to give us the feeling that we are out of control. For example, it's like walking into an empty house. Your mind makes the choice to enter the room. You are in control of that thought and decision, but then for example, you start to feel the feeling of loneliness. You didn't choose that feeling; it came without a mindful thought of choosing it. It seemed like you had no control over the feeling that just entered your body.

Avoiding the feelings that comes from an emotion appears to have become an automatic function of the mind, rather than a choice. We seem to have created defensive strategies that initiate long before conscious choice does to the extent that it doesn't seem that we have a choice. The more emotionally out-of-control we feel, the more our minds set up strategies to control the situation to make us feel safe. The more the feeling of being unloved, unvalued, unheard, unnoticed, disrespected, unliked, the more the mind seems to need to be busy warding off these feelings that come with these emotions.

These are some of the questions that I have asked myself to help me understand the mental emotional process: *What part of ourselves is our mind really protecting and what are the feelings that we don't like feeling? What are the thoughts we don't like thinking and how do these feelings make us feel? Where in the body do we feel them, and why do most of us want to avoid the quietness?*

I believe it is quite easy to find out the answers: just sit somewhere and try and keep your mind quiet, watching the thoughts coming at you. If you have never done this before, your mind will definitely not like sitting in a quiet, still place. It will want to fill up the emptiness with thoughts, ideas and distractions. But what is your mind trying to keep you away from and why doesn't it like this quiet place?

Exercise 20.

Write your answers in your *Breaking Free* journal.

Title your new page: "How To Conquer My Busy Mind."

Find a quiet place where you won't be disturbed, sit comfortably and quietly, and observe the feelings and the stories that sitting quietly evokes.

1. What feelings come up and where do you feel the feelings in your body?

2. See if you can remain still and feel in to where the discomfort is. Just allow yourself to feel into the emotions

119

and feelings and observe this.

3. Inquire into where the origins of these stories and feelings come from in your life.

4. Write down the stories and the feelings that arise.

Summary

I believe conquering an overly busy mind is quite easy, but it does require going into places where the mind doesn't want to go. Take your mind into the quietness, take your mind into the stillness, and discover why the mind doesn't want to be in a quiet place. Having a busy mind is just a distraction to keep you away from one of the most blissful states of consciousness, a place of stillness, peace, contentment and tranquility.

To have control of your mind, you will need to be able to watch the thoughts come and go, and know you have a choice around what you do and how you react to each thought. Remember you are not your thoughts; you are the person watching the thoughts. What has helped me to have a fulfilling, more abundant life with a quieter mind has been my ability to see things differently and by changing my underlying stories. I now know why my mind was so busy. I know the feelings that I didn't want to feel and the stories associated with these fears. I now have no fear of the quietness. It's my friend and place of freedom.

I encourage you to take control of your mind, to grow your mental mastery, be in control of what you think, learn what the stories are keeping you away from having a quiet mind, and learn how to turn your mind off so you can be comfortable with the stillness and quietness.

The easiest way to do this is to meditate each day. To start, try five minutes. That's all. Just five minutes a day. Meditation is a practice so you will need to practice it and see what comes up. Find a simple practice and do it every day. What you will get from a meditation practice will be life and mind changing, literally.

Chapter 22

Is Doing Nothing Really Easy?

I had this limiting belief story that I have been given about working hard - that is, that work is hard, it takes away all your free time, it's a struggle, it's not fun, you *have* to do it, there is no choice, working hard is suffering, and you have to suffer to get ahead. As I see it, most of us have two ways of reacting to a story embedded into a young childhood psyche: to conform or rebel. Which way we go seems to depend on our personality. In my example, I conformed to what my parents taught me. I believed what they said was true and so I worked hard and struggled. Struggling, suffering, and working hard were things I associated with work.

I was good at it, too. I struggled. I worked hard. I struggled again. I worked harder. I even got a job that I didn't like and suffered some more. I was the king of the hard workers, king of the sufferers. I bought a house and then struggled to pay a mortgage, so I worked harder. My parents said, "Struggling makes you appreciate it more." Yeah, right! It resulted in the feeling of being trapped. However, I have had the good fortune of being able to transform this, and I will share exactly how I did later on.

The opposite of the "work hard story" is the "rebel against working" story and the "I don't work hard since I want life to be easy." A person who believes this story may think, "If I don't do much, then I won't have to push myself and suffer, and life will be easy." What if both parts of this story are untrue and that the opposite is, in fact, true? What if not working hard or not working very much isn't easy, but is actually hard and a struggle? Think about it. If you don't work much, you don't make any money. You struggle paying bills. You may not be able to afford good quality food or be able to eat out, have a cup of coffee with a friend in a café, or attend movies, performances, sporting or cultural events. You may not be able to afford petrol, babysitters, or travel. You're probably not going to be able to save anything, and you may not be able to afford to see the dentist, doctor, or optometrist. You may not be able to help others in need, those stricken by disaster, the starving and homeless - hey, maybe because that's you.

It may be *easy*, sort of, but it does sound hard and like struggling to me. I'm not saying that you can't survive without all of these things. Of course you can, but having money can make life a lot easier and less stressful, even for the basic requirements such as food, clothing, and shelter. I know people in this world survive on nothing and are happy, but watch how their happiness grows when they are given more food and clean water.

Instead, what if working hard was fun, easy, and rewarding and could make you happy? Why can't working hard be easy, especially if you love what you do? Can we change the story we have around working? I'm sure we can.

For me, it started with my story about money. How I transformed my story about money took three steps. Firstly, I identified the underlying story I had. I determined these stories by working out how my parents viewed money because no doubt it would be a combination of both their stories. In the case of my mother, she had the "You have to struggle and work hard, and that builds your character" story, and my dad had the "You have to work hard all your life, and it will pay off in the end" story.

Secondly, I had to question the truthfulness of each of their beliefs. For my mum's, I asked: *Does struggling build character?* I decided this was not true, as I know some incredible characters who have never struggled with money. As for my dad's story - his own life answered the truth of his belief story. He worked hard all his life and at fifty years of age contracted cancer and died never getting to spend the money he had been building up.

The third step was to create new empowering stories of how I truly wanted money and wealth to be in my life. My story now is that I have abundance and wealth easily, and money comes freely from anywhere and everywhere. It also comes when I do what I love and when I add value to other people's lives.

You may have been able to save and have done and tried everything you've ever wanted to. What if you've saved enough money and invested it and now have a passive income of $4,000 dollars a week? You have paid off your house, your boat, put your kids through school, traveled to a different country each year with your family, visited your family and friends, supported your favorite aid foundation, and helped make a difference in the world. This life sounds like fun and a bit easier, doesn't it? I'm not saying this is the way people should live their lives; there are many different models and structures for happiness. I'm just saying having money can make it a little easier in certain ways.

One of the main keys to this is having investments that earn you money, a money machine or a so-called "Golden Goose." This is the key to financial freedom but not everybody has been taught how to do this or how it works. This is why rich people are rich and also teach their children these principles.

I have changed my story around working hard and struggling. It's the best thing I ever did. I live with a different sense of freedom now. I believe working is about using my gifts and my skills to their fullest and doing what I love. It's about being creative, being productive, and contributing to other people's lives, living my life to its fullest potential, having fun, and being happy while I do it.

Exercise 21.

Write your answers in your *Breaking Free* journal.

Title a new page: "Working Is Fun And Easy."

1. What are your belief stories about working? Is it easy, or do you have to work hard to get ahead?

2. Do you have a job you love and look forward to doing it each day?

3. What would your ideal job be?

4. What if money wasn't an option, what would you do with your life?

5. If you're not doing it, why aren't you doing it?

6. What excuse did you just make up to justify why you can't do it now?

Summary

Choose the more compelling story: that work is fun and easy. Live an exciting and productive life. Do a job you love. Have fun while working hard. Balance it out by having rest and holidays. Invest money for your future. Have an exceptional and enriching life that includes all aspects of "wealth." Check out the story you have running in the background around work. Imagine working in a job that you love and you look forward to doing it every day. Now go and do it. Inquire into stories you have running in the background that are stopping you. Change it if it is doing you a disservice and is making your life a struggle. If you are already happy about working hard and having fun, living in the present and investing in your future, then I look forward to seeing you in Bali or the Bahamas one day soon.

Chapter 23

What If You Already Live In Paradise?

Growing up, I remember my parents talking about what they would do if they won the lottery. They decided they would go for a holiday to the Bahamas. I had a picture in my head that this was the paradise holiday destination to aspire to.

Then I had a clear insight that I actually already lived on an island paradise, New Zealand and now Bali, Indonesia. For years I thought paradise was someplace else. Why did my parents think paradise was also somewhere else? Was it the "grass is always greener on the other side" notion? Could they not see how blessed they already were to be born and live in New Zealand? Not only that, but we lived in a beautiful place on the East Coast of New Zealand with golden white sandy beaches, hot summers, and the highest number of sunshine hours in the country. Did they not feel happy and think that if they could go somewhere else, they would find happiness there? I'm not sure of the exact reason. But why couldn't they see what they already had?

People all around the world work hard, save their money and come to New Zealand for their island holiday getaways. New Zealand is one of the world's top holiday destinations. Additionally, thousands of people immigrate to New Zealand every year because of the lifestyle, beautiful green landscapes, native forests, breathtaking natural beauty, and its friendly people, which make it a goal destination for many people to live or to holiday - a place to find fun, joy, and happiness, just like my parents' goal was to go to the Bahamas. When you live in a place for a long time, you can take it for granted. Maybe it was just that?

If I look at New Zealand, I see beaches, lakes, rivers, mountains, trees, bush, birds, wildlife, clear air, clean food, clean water, a small population and a predominantly unspoiled country. Sounds like everything you could ever want in an island holiday getaway. New Zealand may not have the year-round tropical temperatures, but we do have great summers. Putting all this aside, why don't we see it that way? Why do New Zealanders go overseas for holidays when they haven't seen all of New Zealand? Many people I know have never been to the South Island, one of the most beautiful islands in the world with amazing snow-covered mountain ranges, rivers, lakes, and forests, beaches, wilderness, solitude, the rawness of the West Coast, beautiful cities, towns, and people.

I realize that not everyone wants the sunny tropical islands for their holidays. For some, it could be a shopping trip to New York, or a foreign culture trip through South America, or a sightseeing trip to Europe. Or like myself, I was brought up believing the goal in life was to go on the ultimate holiday to the Bahamas. I believe the message I got was that fun and happiness were somewhere else, and joy and excitement were attained by going somewhere other than where I lived. The story I picked up was if my parents weren't that happy, then clearly we weren't living in paradise. Paradise must be somewhere else, and where we lived wasn't enough.

Maybe if our lives were already full of joy, inspiration, and happiness, these holidays would just make you feel the same way you already do?

Maybe I needed to ask myself what was it that they wanted and what did I really want in life? For my parents, was it the holiday or a change of scenery and lifestyle? Were they looking for fun, excitement and happiness, something they perceived they didn't already have even though we lived in the end product of other people's desires and dreams? Why were they not insanely happy or content?

Maybe the problem is that the goal of the "holiday in paradise will make you happy" concept is not true. Maybe it doesn't bring you long-lasting joy and a feeling of success? Maybe the novelty of living on a beautiful island wears off, and after a while, it's just another island with golden sandy beaches. And the notion that it will give you eternal happiness is just an illusion, a story or ideal someone has sold us in the advertising brochures for island getaways. Advertising has created an expectation that this holiday will make you happy. I'm not saying these holidays don't make you happy, as they probably do. But is it because your life is so uneventful, uninteresting, unhappy, and unfulfilling? Maybe if your life were already bursting with joy and creativity, love and excitement, these holidays would just make you feel the same way you already do.

I see New Zealand very differently now, and I realize how exceptionally lucky I was to have been born and brought up there. New Zealand has enough food for everyone, free education, great medical support, good weather, a low crime rate, low unemployment, homes for almost everyone, and a welfare system where you get paid even if you don't work. That sounds like a pretty amazing place to live compared to other countries around the world!

So I have to ask myself, why did I always search for happiness outside of myself? I thought happiness was out there somewhere, in some other place, some other town, some other country, or some other paradise. The answer is because that's the example I was given as a child. That's what I was told. That's what I was shown. It might not have been in those exact words, but that's the message I received: Happiness is somewhere else outside of yourself, something to go looking for, something you strive for, and that there is something you have to do in order to get it.

When I was young, I was happy just sitting and playing in a sandpit. How come it takes so much more for my mind to feel happiness and contentment now? When I was young, I didn't think happiness was the answer. I didn't even know there was a question. How come happiness became the goal now? What changed? My heart seems to want love from the outside and my mind seeks fulfillment from the inside. These ideas came from the beliefs of my parents and the beliefs of society, and I now challenge these views to determine whether or not they are actually true.

I believe acceptance of my life and what arises is one of the major keys to happiness and contentment. It's about breaking the story that happiness is outside of yourself. I truly believe happiness is in your own heart.

Exercise 22.

Write your answers in your *Breaking Free* journal.

Title a new page: "I Live In Paradise Every Day."

1. Write down 3 examples of where you would like to be right now rather than where you are in this moment.

2. What is it you think you will get "there" that you don't get where you are right now?

3. What do you think you will feel "there" that you are not feeling now?

4. How could you change your focus and what you are doing right now to get the same feeling as being in the other places?

5. What do you need to do to create that feeling in your life?

6. Imagine being happy and content wherever you are in the world, every minute, every day, without having to go anywhere. How does that feel?

Summary

I know now contentment comes from gratitude for what I have right here and right now, and that happiness comes from the paradise in my own heart, not from some possible distant future. I know that seeking joy outside of myself is a short-lived illusion. I believe happiness is a choice. I can be happy in the Bahamas and I can be happy in a cardboard box. It's my choice. As I said to a friend the other day: pick happy. Why not? You could always pick the other one if you want.

Chapter 24

Is Having An Accident Fate?

I was involved in an accident where a jogger ran out in front of me while I was driving through a set of traffic lights on my motorbike. It wasn't the accident that I found fascinating, or who was in the right or wrong, or the damage to the motorbike I was riding, or the injuries to both of us (we both were lucky enough to get away with a few minor bruises and painful bones) - it was the timing.

Instead of waiting at the pedestrian crossing, she crossed in-between two stopped cars that were waiting for the lights to change at the precise time when I was driving down the road. I don't know what she had been doing before; maybe she had stopped to do up her shoelaces or change the music on her iPod. Maybe she simply left home five minutes later than normal. All these things happened and culminated in her being at the exact place at that exact time.

Then there are the circumstances that led me to be driving past at that exact point in time. I had stopped to talk to some students and fellow tutors after class. I then got onto my motorbike and traveled only fifty meters down the road, and at the precise second, I drove past a line of cars, the woman ran out in front of me. I crashed into her at the same moment I saw her. No warning, no time to brake, no time to swerve.

The timing was exact, and I had absolutely no chance of missing her. If I had said one more sentence to the students or if I had to wait for a car coming down the road before I pulled out into the line of traffic, just one more second, I would not have hit her. The timing for our paths to cross was down to a millisecond. Funnily enough, accidents usually come down to a discussion about who was in the wrong or the right, or it's a dispute about who is going to pay for the repairs and damage. For me, it was about timing and understanding that there is no such thing as coincidence.

Was this an accident or fate? Was it bad luck or some kind of divine intervention? Was it karma? I do believe accidents happen for a reason, and there is always an invaluable learning available to us concerning the situation and circumstances of the accident. Accidents can also provide us with an amazing reflection or insight as to what is happening in our lives at the time. If they are about learning a lesson, what was the lesson? In my case, was it that I'm not in control of my destiny and there is something much bigger working behind the scenes? Is our whole life like this, just one big accident or incident waiting to happen? Are there lessons behind every event, either planned or not planned, in our lives or is life just a series of random coincidences? Is there such a thing as destiny or divine providence or just good luck and bad luck, or good karma or bad karma? Do we just live in chaos?

I think there are probably just as many theories about this as there are theories about what happens after we die. A Chinese friend said to me once that some Chinese people use whichever philosophy fits the situation. They either use a Taoist, Buddhist, or Confucianism teaching to understand and explain why something happens. I don't know what the answer to this is. I just have a belief that there is a reason certain things happen so I am able to make some sort of sense out of these random confusing events.

After deep introspection, I believe the learning around the accident for me was to let go of a story about things being fair or unfair. It's an old belief I've had that things need to be fair. But maybe the reality is that things just happen in the world, and it's not about whether they are fair or not. My story in this instance was that it was unfair because I didn't cause the accident, and I damaged my friend's motorbike.

It's not fair that my friend's bike was not insured and the person who caused the accident had no money to fix it. This all seemed a little unfair to me, as I didn't cause this to happen, and I was going to have to pay for the bike's repairs.

Are they all just stories of who is right in a situation and who is wrong? Is the truth a totally different story, or is the truth really just that she just made a simple mistake and, of course, didn't really want this to happen, and it just so happened that her mind was very busy, she was potentially being impatient, and she really didn't have the money to pay for the damages while I did have the money to fix the bike without any problem? All I needed to do was let go of the "fair or unfair" story.

I wonder what the lesson was for the jogger as to why it happened? Was it about getting out of her busy mind and focusing more on what's happening around her or learning that she doesn't need to hurry all the time, or that maybe she can slow down and it is good to wait and have patience?

Who knows what was happening for her at work, in her home life, or with her health? So who am I to judge another's actions? The lesson I received from the accident was an invaluable one for me. I know you may all have your own points of view on this subject, but this is good food for thought, especially about your beliefs around fair and unfair, right or wrong, justice and injustice.

Do things just happen in the world beyond our control, and is there a freedom in that? However we see it, we do have a choice as to how we react to everything that happens, and that is empowering.

Exercise 23.

Write your answers in your *Breaking Free* journal.

Title a new page: "Nothing Happens In The World By Accident."

1. Think of a time in your life when something happened that was completely out of your control. Write down the event and how you reacted to the situation at the time.

2. How did you feel at the time?

3. Were these feelings empowering or disempowering?

4. How could you have reacted differently if you knew there was a lesson to learn, no matter how difficult it may have appeared at the time?

Summary

Step back to gain perspective and see the bigger picture and the lessons that arise from situations or "accidents." These situations are an amazing opportunity to grow and learn.

Stories About What We Think Other People Should Do For Us

Chapter 25

The People Pleaser

The term "People Pleaser" is sometimes used in the psychological field to describe a person who does things to please people in their life in order to get people to like them. I know this one well, as my parents taught me how to be a people pleaser at an early age. I was taught that having people like you was important. This idea was reinforced by comments from my parents like "Don't do that. What will people think of you?" and also by the comments and judgments of other people I overheard. I grew up thinking it was normal for people to talk about me and judge my behavior. Getting people to like me and to think I was a good person became a key driving goal in my life. I thought it is just what you do. My parents may not agree that it was their motive to teach me how to be a people pleaser, but their unconscious words, actions, comments and behavior certainly influenced me. If I were to say and do things that other people agreed with, I would be seen as a good person. To not disagree or do anything that somebody could judge you on seemed very important to me. I questioned this belief later in life. Was it really one of my goals to get people to like me? Probably not.

Was the people-pleasing just another way of surviving in a harsh world? A world where there seemed to be many judgments, comparisons, opinions, and beliefs on how we should or should not behave and live our lives? People-pleasing seems to be just another way to feel loved, cared for, understood, and listened to, which would ultimately make us feel okay about ourselves. But it brings up another question: Why did I need to feel loved, cared for, understood, and heard to make me feel okay about myself?

I witnessed myself becoming a different person in various circles of friends. For example, I would play a certain character with my rugby friends and another one with my army mates. I was a certain character with my old school friends, and when it came to women, I was another completely different character again. They all seemed to like me; well, at least, I think they did, but none of them knew the real "Peter." I had lots of friends from many circles that didn't know each other.

I remember my Taiji teacher at the time asking me, "What would happen if you were the same person in all of these groups?"

I remember my reply vividly. I said, "They wouldn't like me!"

He asked me, "Is it your goal to get everybody to like you?"

Of course, I replied, "Yes."

He asked me, "What if they don't like you?"

And to my shock, I replied, "I can make them like me."

It was like a lead balloon when I heard these words come out of my mouth. I was so embarrassed. I couldn't believe I had just said that, but I did, and I believed it, too.

Who did these people really like? Did they like the different characters I made up in my play of life? Could they see underneath that? Why didn't I think I was good enough just being myself, and for that matter, who was the real me anyway? Which one of these characters whom I portrayed was the real me? Was I none of them? Was I someone else? I remember the actor Peter Sellers saying that he had acted in so many different parts that he had trouble remembering his true character. Who, then, was the real me behind all the masks? Can the real "Peter Caughey" please stand up? I would have if I could have, but I didn't really know who that was at that time. After this series of questions, I set about discovering who I was. I decided to ask my family and friends, which took courage and revealed some interesting aspects of myself that I couldn't see. I did some reading and discovered that there were many parts to my personality and character, but they all had a common thread running through all of them. The common thread was essentially me.

I quite often suggest to people if you want to have a glimpse of your possible character traits to get your astrological star chart done, which you can do online, and even get an evolutionary horoscope reading done by a reputable astrologer.

I have listed a number of resources below for your information:

- Astrology: http://www.astro.com

- Chinese Horoscope: http://www.suzannewhite.com
- Mayan Astrology: http://www.astrodreamadvisor.com/
- Numerology: Dan Millman's book, The Life We Were Born to Live and The Secret Language of Birthdays by Gary Goldschneider: https://www.thesecretlanguage.com/check/birthdate/

By the time you have read through all this information, you will have a good overview of your possible character traits, and then you can confirm it by asking your friends if they feel that is true for you.

Welcome to you! While in essence you know who you are, I believe it's good to learn more about yourself and your possibilities.

I think it's normal to want people to like you. Even on Facebook, the term "like" is used. You "like" a comment or you "like" a photo or you "like" a Facebook page. It's difficult not to like being "liked. There may be an easier way of feeling better about yourself than basing your self-image on what other people think of you. It reminds me of the saying which you may have heard, "What other people think of you is none of your business.

Exercise 24.

Write your answers in your *Breaking Free* journal.

Title a new page: "I Love And Approve Of Myself, And I Don't Need Anyone To Like Me."

1. Do you want people to like you?

2. How does it make you feel when people like you?

3. What do you want people to like about you?

4. Do you really need people to like you?

5. Do you like and accept yourself?

Summary

Not needing people to like you is a great way of building self-esteem and self-respect. I have done a lot of work around this subject to break free from this story, and yet I still catch myself from time to time wanting people to like me. I encourage you to find an affirmation that helps you to break your story around needing people to like you. One of the affirmations that I say each day is:

"I refuse to give the power of how I feel to other people."

Sometimes old needs and habits take a while to break. I believe the more I love and accept myself for who I am, the less I need others to like me. There is a beautiful freedom in that.

Chapter 26

You Should Be What I Think You Should Be!

One of the stories I have painted for myself is that the reason I am here is to "learn as much as I can before I die." I'm not quite sure where this came from - probably some spiritual teaching or book I read. The truth is I really don't know why I'm here or why I was born into this life with the parents I have, with my sister, or my children. All of my personal views as to why I'm here are based on my beliefs and theories. I don't have a problem with these theories and beliefs; it is ultimately what inspires me to get out of bed in the morning. Here's the thing, though: I think everyone should think like I do and that everyone's goals and reason for living on our earth at this time should be the same as mine, and I'm sure if they were, I would be happy; the world would be a better place while also proving that my beliefs are, in fact, true.

I'm guessing you're thinking there are some cracks in my story.

I realize everyone individually has their own unique set of beliefs and theories as to why they are here. So why do I judge people when their beliefs and theories aren't the same as mine? In fact, I don't even know why I made up the story in the first place. Why did I create the story that "my life's journey is to learn as much as I can?" Maybe I made this story up to give myself a life purpose? What if it's not true? Oh dear, now what am I going to do? What am I really here for? Is there any reason at all? This story has helped me bring myself into the present moment, as that seems to be the only place I know of that is actually true. The present moment is right here, right now.

I used to belong to a men's support group that met weekly. I suddenly found myself getting frustrated and annoyed that some of the people weren't getting through their "stuff." Then I realized that the reason I was going to these meetings and the reasons other people were going to the meetings were completely different. Once I was able to accept that they had different reasons than mine, all of my judgment and frustration dissipated. I realized that I couldn't expect others to do what I thought they should do and that my opinions were right for me, but not necessarily for others.

I have learned that we are all different with different beliefs, standards, perceptions, and views. We don't think the same or believe the same things. Understanding this fact has helped me remove all the judgment and expectations I put on people. If we all accept one another and ourselves for our individuality and have kindness and compassion for all human beings, it may be a very different world.

Exercise 25.

Write your answers in your *Breaking Free* journal.

Title a new page: "I Accept Myself And Everybody Else The Way They Are."

> 1. Write a list of some of the expectations that you have for others.

For example:

a. How do I think a good friend should behave?

b. How do I think a good boss should behave?

c. What I do I think an intimate partner should do for me?

d. How do I think children should behave?

2. Are these expectations true? What proof do you have that they are true?

3. Do the people in your life know that you have these expectations for them?

4. What would it be like to have no expectations for these people and yourself?

Summary

I feel that I was confined to my beliefs and opinions about people and was locked into defined viewpoints and a place with no flexibility. Discovering this has given me much more space and freedom, and I don't seem to have so many expectations of people anymore. I also have a lot more understanding and acceptance for myself and others. This, in turn, has given me more contentment and peace. It seems to make communication with other people a lot easier. I am me, and you are you. It sounds a lot less complicated that way, doesn't it?

Try to see people the way they truly are, without any expectations or judgments. We are all just different, and that is the truth.

Chapter 27

The Duck That Didn't Say Thank You

This is an old story that happened to me a while ago when living in Auckland, New Zealand. Like most mornings, I would go down to my local nature reserve to do my Taiji training. It was just me, the ducks, geese, and a few joggers. Watching these birds, I learned many things, and this lesson is one I would like to share with you.

One day just before training, I saw a very sickly looking duck with most of its feathers missing sitting in a muddy patch, not moving. I felt sorry for her, but I didn't know what to do. I picked her up, and put her in the big pond and hoped that she just needed to be back in the water with the other ducks and that would fix her. After I finished my training, which took about an hour, I went back to the pond hoping she had swum away with the other ducks. I couldn't see her, and I thought, *Great! Now she is not my problem or concern. I looked down and at my feet the duck was sitting motionless and too weak to raise her head. I thought, Damn! Now what am I going to do?*

I picked her up and put her on the grass. I sat down beside her, talked to her, and stroked her back. During this process, I witnessed my mind working out all the ways to get out of this position. *Oh well*, I thought. *Ducks die all the time; it's not my responsibility. Maybe somebody else will come and look after her.*

My mind was working so fast to come up with a reason why it

wasn't my responsibility to help her. But as I sat there looking at the poor defenseless duck, I realized that this hadn't happened by chance, so I picked her up, took her home, and made a cage for her to help protect her.

On the way home, a woman stopped me and told me what to feed the duck and how to help her. What a coincidence - out of all the people in Auckland that morning in the park was a woman who knew exactly how to help sick ducks - or was it? I must admit, I didn't think the duck was going to survive. She couldn't even stand up. After a couple days of spoon-feeding her and using the recipe the women had given me, she started to eat the food I put in a bowl in front of her. I noticed that after a few more days, she could hold up her head. I fed and talked to her each day. After about a week, I woke up and went out to feed her, and she was standing up! It was a very cool feeling. I kept her for another week, and during this time all her feathers started to grow back. She started spreading her wings and flapping them and even started pecking at me when I fed her. The time to release her had come.

I put her in a box and carried her down to the pond for the big release back into the wild. It felt like one of those Walt Disney wildlife films: I get to the pond, place the box down, open it up, pick her up, and put her in the water. She starts to swim, shaking her head and tail before swimming off into the distance. I said my goodbyes as she swam away, but she didn't look back once to acknowledge or thank me. She just swam off. I sat there, feeling sadness. I had seen all these wildlife programs where the animal turned back and their eyes met with their savior or they came back for a final pat to say goodbye. Not my duck. With my duck, I got nothing. As I sat there with a feeling of emptiness, I realized that the message in this encounter was not about acknowledgment. It was about doing what I knew was the right thing to do in my heart.

The whole incident taught me not to have expectations when I do something for another being. Unconditional love is a one-way street; you give with no guarantees or expectations that it will be returned.

(A funny side note: while I was sitting by the duck at the pond, a little boy and his mother walked by. They had seen me practicing my Taiji, and the little boy said to his mum, "Hey mum, how come that man is patting that duck?" His mother replied, "He's a Taiji guy, and they can do that kind of thing." It made me smile; little did they know, the duck couldn't move.)

Exercise 26.

Write your answers in your *Breaking Free* journal.

Title a new page: "I Give Freely Without Wanting Anything Back."

1. When you give something to somebody, do you expect something back, even a "Thank you?"

2. Can you give something away unconditionally even as an act of kindness?

3. Today, go and give or do something for somebody and

want nothing back. Witness how this makes you feel and then write it down in your *Breaking Free* journal.

Summary

Helping the duck was not about getting something; it was about giving something. Imagine if everybody simply did things for another and didn't want anything back in return nor craved any form of self-gratification. I think the world would be a much more considerate, loving, and generous place. Thank you, Mrs. Duck, for the lesson in humility.

Chapter 28

Do You Give The Power Of How You Feel To Someone Else?

Why do we give the power of how we feel to someone else? This is a great and complicated question that I have been asking myself. If I want somebody to love me, to make me feel wanted, loved and appreciated, respected and accepted, then they become the holder to the keys to whether I feel happy or not. I am literally handing over all my personal power. I don't know about you, but I certainly don't want to rely on somebody else loving me in order for me to feel okay about myself.

What if they are having a bad day? Is it likely that they are then going to turn around and give me love, kindness, and attention? Probably not. They will probably be feeling empty themselves, which then results in my own feelings of feeling unloved and uncared for because they are unable to give me what I wanted or needed. It doesn't seem logical to hand over my own sense of self-esteem to another person. It's irrelevant whether it is my children, my partner, or my parents - by handing over my own power, I am unable to determine my level of happiness or quality of life. Instead, I can see myself being constantly disappointed, hurt, and lonely.

So how do we take it back, this power we have given away? How do we become self-determining leaders of our own feelings? Easy.

153

Refuse to give the power of how you feel to someone else. Know that you are the only person who makes you feel sad, happy, angry, resentful or joyful; you are the captain of your own ship. Start by loving yourself. Love your character. Love the different parts of your personality. Love your body, as it is the one you've been given. Love your style. Love your creativity. Love your sense of humor. Love the food you like. But most of all, love and accept the things you don't like about yourself: the inner child that spits the dummy when you don't get what you want or feels put down or rejected or ignored. Love the shadow aspect of yourself, the one who reacts to people or situations, the one who may attack other people when you don't get your own way or when you feel hurt. By loving and accepting all sides, even our shadow and darker sides, we can finally be free from judgment, not only of others but of ourselves.

The truth is that another person can't make you do anything; you choose to react the way you react at any given moment. To love and accept yourself unconditionally, I believe, is one of the hardest things to do. I seem to carry a lot of judgment about others and myself. Love the part that judges another's actions. Love the part that judges your own actions. Love the part of you that sometimes wishes everyone would just go away.

Often the things we don't tolerate in others are what we don't tolerate in ourselves. It's hard to love ourselves unconditionally even though we want others to accept and love us unconditionally. Maybe if we could love ourselves unconditionally, then we wouldn't judge ourselves so much?

I have observed this myself and in my own actions. The more I love and accept myself for who I really am, the good and the not-so-good bits, and see them as not good or bad but just parts of my personality, then the judgment of others also subsides and the acceptance of others grows. I realize we are all just doing the best we can in the chaos, and because we are all so different from each other, how can I judge another anyway? Who can ever be perfect, whatever perfect looks like?

It's like comparing pine and oak trees; they are both trees. But that's about all. So now I've taken back the power of how I feel, and I encourage you to do the same. I make my own self-determining choices about how I feel, which has given me more freedom to be myself and not care so much what others think about me.

Here is a practical exercise to do to see if you are giving your power away to others. Next time you are talking to someone, ask yourself, "Do I want something from this person? Do I want them to hear me? Do I want them to like me? Do I want them to think I'm a good person?"

After recognizing what you wanted (if anything) from the person, say to yourself, "I want nothing from this person, but I can listen freely to them; I am already happy and content, and I need nothing from them." See how you feel after the short process.

Exercise 27.

Write your answers in your *Breaking Free* journal.

Title a new page: "I Love And Accept Myself Unconditionally."

1. Do you love yourself unconditionally?

2. What parts about yourself do you like? List them.

3. What parts about yourself do you not like? List them.

4. What would it be like if you accepted the parts you don't like about yourself? How would you feel?

Summary

Accept yourself for who you are. Be in control of how you feel. Be responsible for your own actions. Be in charge of the choices you make. It's your life. What do you want to do with it? You're in control of it. Be empowered and be free.

Chapter 29

Why Do I Want People to Listen to Me?

I observed myself reacting in a strange behavioral pattern one afternoon when my wife Josephine and I had friends over for lunch. During our conversation, I witnessed myself wanting to tell one of our friends just how much I knew about a certain subject. I also observed that she wanted to tell me what she knew. It seemed to turn into a competition about who knew the most. I wondered to myself, *Why am I doing this? What was triggering me? Was it the need to get her to understand that I knew more than her about the subject? What was I trying to prove?"*

At one stage of our conversation, she corrected something I said, and I witnessed myself justifying my comment. Even though I was aware of what I was doing, I found it difficult to stop; I wanted to keep playing the game. I talked to Josephine later that night after our guests had left. She laughed and said it was hard to get a word in between our friend and me. She asked me why I needed to keep making my point, which was a great question, and we talked about how I was feeling.

It took a little while to uncover the reasons I was reacting so much to the conversation. I realized this was the same dynamic that I had with my mother. I always seemed to want to prove to her how much I knew and had learned in my life. Even at 50, I was still trying to get her to listen to me and obtain her approval - constantly trying to prove to her that I wasn't stupid. This dynamic stemmed back to when I was a child. As a young person, I remember my mum being very bright. She was very good at spelling; she loved reading books and was excellent at writing. She had worked as a secretary and shorthand typist for a large company when she was a young woman. She was a very good wordsmith and also loved crossword puzzles. Well, I was the opposite. I always felt inadequate with my English comprehension and grammar because of my dyslexia, which made reading and writing difficult for me. I now believe that, as a child, somewhere in my mind was a story that my mum thought I was dumb and that I wasn't trying hard enough, hence my need to prove I wasn't stupid.

I remember her saying comments to me like, "I've been around a lot longer than you; I know a lot more than you," and "How do I get through to you?" "Don't you understand anything?" "You just don't get it," "You think you know everything, but you don't." So I spent a lot of time trying to seek my mother's approval.

Even as an adult, if I had an argument with my mother, she would use the ploy of putting me down so that she would win the argument. She'd base her argument on an assumption that I didn't know anything; this would immediately take me into my wounded child and completely disempowered me. I would feel like a naive little boy. I know she didn't do this consciously; it was just the strategy she used to win arguments, which resulted in her building up her own ego and self-esteem. I would start saying things to her to prove that I knew things, but really I was seeking her approval. I was powerless in this place, and I certainly didn't feel good about myself.

When I realized this pattern, I chose to consciously change the dynamic between my mother and me. We still had disagreements, but not about who was right and who was wrong or who knew the most.

I believe our parents are one of the biggest potential sources of growth that we are gifted in our lifetime, and they are the key to the origins of the majority of our stories about what we think life is. They have influenced our behavior, reactions, responses, viewpoints, and beliefs. Once we become aware and conscious of our own patterning, we have the power to change.

So back to lunch with our friends. Here I am playing out the same approval-seeking game with our guest. I realize now that we were both playing the game, both seeking appreciation from each other, both wanting to be heard, both wanting to be respected for our knowledge. If I had questioned her about her childhood, I imagine she would have a similar dynamic that I did of not being heard by one or both parents.

This was such a great experience and a very useful lesson for me to learn. I don't need to tell people what I know - if, in fact, I know anything anyway. Ultimately what I think I know stems from my own personal opinions, beliefs, and points of view. Now when I see my friend, I am committed to listening to her wisdom and giving her the gift of being and feeling heard.

I know that when talking to somebody, I may want acknowledgment for my views and ideas, and I realize that, at the same time, the other person probably may want me to see and hear them, too. If there is some truth in this, then how much do I really listen to others when they are speaking? I sometimes catch myself thinking of what I want to say next and am not really listening to what they're saying; I'm just waiting for a gap in the conversation so I can whip in my views and insert my knowledge on the subject. I understand now that one of the biggest insights into communication is to practice active listening and not talking.

I have three daily affirmations that may resonate with you when facing this subject:

- *I love and approve of myself.*
- *I'm free to express my thoughts and opinions or keep them to myself.*
- *I don't need people to listen to me.*

Exercise 28.

Write your answers in your *Breaking Free* journal.

Title a new page: "I Don't Need People To Listen To Me."

1. Why do you want people to listen to you?

2. How does it feel if you don't need people to listen to you?

3. Are you a good listener?

4. Do you really need someone to listen to you in order for you to feel okay about yourself?

Summary

People do not need to agree with you for you to be a knowledgeable person. Remember, sometimes it's just your opinion or point of view, which is true for you but not necessarily for others, and it may not actually be true. Free yourself from needing anybody to listen to you.

I use a saying that was given to me, which I think is very wise: "Say what you mean, mean what you say, or say nothing at all."

Sometimes saying nothing is the best option. Be free to speak your truth and remember that it is only your truth, not necessarily everybody else's.

Chapter 30

The Underlying Story Is More Important To Focus On If You Want to be Free

I woke up one day and found myself looking inside, which sounds pretty weird, but I can tell you it was a very profound experience. I clearly saw my need to be loved and a need to have other people see who I really am. I realized we all may need and seek the same or very similar things in our lives: to be loved and seen.

I noticed that if I didn't feel loved, I felt a gap, an emptiness. I observed myself trying to fill this gap to make myself feel better and to avoid feeling the sense of isolation. I have looked at people and noticed that we all seem to have our own ways of gap-filling to avoid feeling the emotional sensations and feelings we don't like, whether it's through food, alcohol, drugs, shopping, chocolate, sugar, friends, movies, books, or Facebook.

Some people call these "addictions" and use them to avoid feeling pain or emptiness. Some of these addictions are clearly healthier than others, such as being addicted to exercise or healthy food. Some of my own gap fillers are food, movies, and motorsports. However, the main one for me is to simply keep busy. I observed that when I was by myself it triggered a feeling of not being loved.

My personal challenge was to sit quietly and observe the feelings that arose in the quietness and stillness. This silence was very uncomfortable to me. I observed myself just wanting to do something - anything - to take away this feeling. I discovered later that this place was a true place of existence, a place where I could see all things, a place of clarity and tranquility, but no one told me that back then, so I just associated it with pain.

I have learned from my own experiences that one of the ways I felt the silence and feeling of emptiness, or the gap, was created by my thoughts that I'm not good enough, which trigger another underlying story: if I'm not *good enough,* no one will love me. These are false belief stories in many ways; firstly, that the experience of the silence and the emptiness is a bad thing to feel; secondly, that you have to be good enough for someone to love you; and thirdly, who said someone is meant to love you? I wish somebody had mentioned this to me earlier in my life. It would have saved me lots of unnecessary hours in the counselor's office. Mind you, if I had have known the truth of why I kept myself so busy filling up the hole so I couldn't feel the feeling of emptiness, maybe nothing in the house would have been repaired. I'm not saying that doing things and being busy are wrong. I think being creative, innovative, and expanding knowledge and skills are great! I'm just saying the driving force behind my reasons for being busy were not necessarily beneficial. I encourage you to examine what your background story is that's driving the need to be good enough or the need to be loved.

Now, as for the other part of wanting people to see me, this stems back to my childhood and wanting my parents to see me. I remember how I got their attention either by doing well at sports, at school, or being naughty because negative attention is better than no attention. I remember a great story that taught me this very lesson. I was taking an afterschool sports program in my early 30's and there were a couple of kids who would run around and never do what I asked them to do. I was working with a former schoolteacher, and she asked if she could help me out with this. I gladly agreed. She pointed out that when I called for everyone to sit on the stage, young Rebecca would always very quickly sit on the stage with her arms folded and waited while I chased the two boys around. My colleague suggested I compliment how well Rebecca was sitting on the stage, which I did, and two seconds later, the two boys were sitting on the stage with their arms folded beside her. I turned to Jude and said, "No, it can't be that easy," and she said, "Attention is attention; there are just different ways of getting it." Thanks, Jude for the great lesson; I have remembered it to this day.

In Traditional Chinese Medicine, it is believed to be more valuable to find the root cause of the problem and then eliminate it rather than to treat the symptom. I think it is easy to be sidetracked by an external feeling and emotion and miss the underlining and deeper cause. In Traditional Chinese Medicine, if you treat the source of the problem, the symptom will go away. In using my example, how can you feel the emptiness when there is no such thing as being good enough and you don't need someone to love you?

When you truly love yourself and you feel truly good enough in yourself and you accept the person who you are, how can there be emptiness? This has also brought up a very valuable point, which is a false belief story that somebody outside of yourself is meant to love you and that getting this love from someone would ultimately make you happy.

When I became aware that I had the story and a belief that somebody is meant to love me and see me, I realized that by holding onto these stories, I was actually giving away the power of how I feel to someone else. I now believe people aren't here to give us love, but they are here for us to experience the feeling of what it is like to give love away. This is one of the many gifts people give to us: they provide an opening and an opportunity for us to experience, feel, see, and give away the love that is already within us.

Exercise 29.

Write your answers in your *Breaking Free* journal.

Title a new page: "I Can See The True Underlying Cause Of All My Stories."

1. How do you fill the gap when you are feeling the emptiness? Write a list of all the ways you fill up the gap when you are feeling emptiness.

2. What feelings come up when you are by yourself in the quietness, and where do you feel it in your body?

3. Would you like to change the way you see this place so that it becomes a place where you get peace and quiet, a place of quality time for yourself?

4. How could you use this quiet time in a more nurturing way towards yourself? For example, meditating, taking a long walk in nature, writing in your journal, listening to music or playing an instrument, or anything that helps you experience contentment and the joy of being alone in your soul in the quietness.

Summary

It is not the symptom (in my example, emptiness), but the cause (for me, a feeling of not being loved or that nobody is there for you) that was most critical for me to investigate. Discovering the underlying story is one of the true secrets of breaking your limiting belief stories. It's not what you do; it's why you do it. What is the true motivation, the driving force behind your behavior and beliefs and how you see the world? Discovering this is the doorway to freedom.

Break free from your limiting stories, and see the world with a new set of eyes, fearlessly and with an open heart.

Chapter 31

Is It Really About Sacrifice?

One night I had a dream that a person was dying from a strange contagious disease and was quarantined in a hospital. One of the scientists at the hospital had made a device that could kill the disease by refracting light. The main problem was the device, when turned on, would kill any other person in the room other than the patients. The other major problem was that someone had to be in the room to manually align the device, and the room had to be sealed before the machine could safely be turned on.

Five scientists all volunteered to be the one to be sealed in the room with the patient and operate the light refractor; however, only one scientist was required. To make the decision easy, they had another person fill up five glasses of water and put a tasteless tranquilizer in one of the glasses. All five scientists chose a glass of water to drink. The one who collapsed from the tranquilizer was carried into the air-locked room with the patient and then the room was sealed. They knew when the scientist woke up that he or she would understand what had happened and that they were the one required to carry out the task of aligning the light refractor and ending his or her own life.

When the scientist woke in my dream, it was a man. He stood up and looked through the glass window at the other scientists. No words were spoken, as they all understood the choice of offering their own life for the dying person. Once he had lined up the lights on the machine, he turned and looked at his colleagues one last time, holding eye contact for a moment. As he switched on the machine, he knew he only had one minute left to live but was at peace with his decision. He knew that if this device worked, it could save thousands of human lives, not just the person on the table. He understood the need to make this sacrifice, to help other people, and that sometimes it may mean giving up your life. After he had switched on the machine, he sat down smiling to himself. The patient survived.

We hear of this many times: people giving up their lives to save others. It must be buried deep in our psyche somewhere. It is known as altruism. While we are probably more inclined to do this for our family or friends, would we do it for a total stranger? Many have. There seems to be a deep primal need to help people, to rescue people, to save them. We all like seeing the fireman go into the burning building and bring out people alive. Many a soldier has gone back to save his friend; many women have saved a child's life at the cost of their own.

Maybe we intrinsically hope that someone would be willing to die for us or rescue us because that is what we want for ourselves and we find ourselves willing to do this for another person, even if it is for someone we don't know? Is it an inherent part of our nature that wants to save and help people? When somebody is drowning, we want to help. When somebody is choking, we want to help. When there is a car accident, people want to help. I am not saying that we all want to help in these situations, but enough people do to make me ask this question. What is it inside of us? Part of our instinct and a deeper urge to protect? Is it a belief story we are taught? An instinct to survive? If it is an instinct to survive, why would some people give their lives for another? Is it an instinctive animal behavior to save the herd or species even though it is detrimental to the individual?

I love discovering what drives me and others - what drives instincts, choices, behavior. Is it something we are taught or is it an inner knowing we are born with? Did your parents teach you that if someone is drowning, you should try and save them?

To truly know yourself is to know what you would do and how you would respond in different situations and to know why you are making this choice and what is driving it. However, there is always the great unknown factor that makes humans unique, different, and special, and that is when we react from a deeper inner source. One that doesn't have a mind, motive, or reason. I point to this in this chapter to bring light to the unknown, our unknown reactions without seeming rhyme or reason, and the unexplainable. There are many things that we do as well as behaviors, which can be explained by our childhood environment, parenting, schooling, or just our personality or character. However, there are some things that can't be explained.

Some may call it the "X" factor, but I call it the true essence of our souls. I think one of our true missions in life is to reveal and experience this part of ourselves. The part of ourselves that would dive into the water to save a total stranger from drowning. The part that would go into a burning car to pull someone out. That's what I'm interested in. Where does that live inside of us? I'm not saying that we should all do this, as not wanting to go into a burning car is equally important, and there is no right or wrong response. It's about knowing and understanding ourselves. It's not about judgment, but awareness.

Exercise 30.

Write your answers in your *Breaking Free* journal.

Title a new page: "I Like Asking For Help For Myself And I Like Helping Other People."

1. If an elderly lady fell over in front of you, would you stop to help her up?

2. If somebody were drowning, would you want to save him or her even if you weren't a confident swimmer? Would the urge to save them still be there?

3. Why do you think that you would want to help and rescue them? What do you think drives you to help other people?

Summary

Some people just like helping others for no reason and some people like helping others as they would like to help themselves, which could be for many reasons. There is no right or wrong with this; it's about discovering who you are and loving and accepting yourself unconditionally. There are many people in the world, and they are all different, including you. I think one of the most useful concepts to understand is that it's not what you do but *why* you do it. What drives it, what lives underneath it, what is your motivation, and what is your goal for doing it? I believe understanding yourself and what drives you can lead to a more conscious life and can help you make more informed choices.

Chapter 32

Why Don't I Like People Helping Me?

This chapter carries on from the previous chapter, "Is It Really About Sacrifice?" which discusses the innate human instinct to want to help others. This chapter is about the other side of the coin: *not* wanting to accept help from others. I have observed that some people do not like accepting and receiving help from other people. There may be a myriad of different stories as to why, and there are enough people who do this that made me inquire into it, not only for myself but for others.

This behavior seems to be strangely prevalent in people who like to give to others themselves. It is more difficult to determine the reason why other people don't like receiving help from others without asking them than it is to determine our own reasons. So I asked myself: *Why don't I like receiving help from others?* My answer came back pretty quickly. In my case, it was a story that if I accepted help, it meant I was too dumb to work it out myself and that I was useless because I couldn't do it on my own. I also realized I had another belief that only needy people needed or asked for help. What if others think you are now obligated to them?

I remember people offering me help and me saying, "No, no. It's okay. I can do it myself." Or, "It's okay; I can get it myself." On other occasions, I remember saying after someone offered me help, "I don't want to trouble you," and they would say, "It's no trouble," and I'd refuse again, saying, "No, I will be okay."

Why couldn't I accept help? I like to help people, but I didn't like accepting help, let alone asking for it. I was now aware I had another story in my head saying that asking for help was even worse than accepting somebody's offer to help. I thought into how I would feel if I asked for help, and I immediately felt a feeling of total incompetence, of defeat and worthlessness. Wow! No wonder I never asked for help.

I feel it isn't always important to know where these stories come from. What was more important for me was to recognize and accept that none of these stories are actually true. I had my breakthrough on this subject when my Taiji master asked me, "Why don't you like people helping you?" I hadn't even thought it was a problem until he asked. I thought about it and gave him the answer that I have already mentioned.

"Do you like helping other people?" he asked.

"Yes," I said.

"How does it feel to help somebody?"

"It makes me feel great," I answered.

"When somebody tries to give to you and you say no, you deny them an opportunity to feel that feeling, too," he said.

I felt so bad that I was taking away somebody else's chance to feel that. He explained it in a different way using the principles of Taiji energy exchange. He said that the concept of giving and receiving is an aspect in many religious teachings. He then explained it using the Christian concept of the Holy Spirit. He explained that when you give help or love to someone, the Holy Spirit comes through you and out to the other person. He continued, "By not accepting their help or love, you stop them feeling the Holy Spirit or divine energy coming through them."

This made me feel terrible. To this day, I remember that lesson, and I now accept help, gifts, and good intentions from people gladly.

Helping people feels so great, so why would I ever deny anybody else the opportunity to feel that? I also believe helping people is one of the greatest sources of happiness and contentment in life.

Exercise 31.

Write your answers in your *Breaking Free* journal.

Title a new page: "I Like Asking And Accepting Help From Other People."

1. Do you like accepting help from others? Yes or no?

2. If you answered "No," what story or stories do you have about accepting help?

3. Are these stories really true?

4. Can you accept people helping you knowing that it gives them a chance to feel divine energy in their hearts?

Summary

I have helped many people with this issue over the years, and I call it an "issue" very loosely. I've helped and encouraged them to see it another way, a way of gratitude and acceptance. I have helped people to disempower their belief around receiving help, and I've helped them to understand that receiving help is a true sign of strength and courage and that sometimes we just need help and it's okay. By accepting people's help, you allow them to feel the spirit of giving, and what a beautiful gift that is to give to somebody.

Chapter 33

The Greatest Deception of Them All

One of the greatest deceptions I believe is that someone in the world is meant to love you. I think you will take a major step forward in developing emotional mastery in your life if you can break free from this belief. I believe it is one of the key steps in understanding your emotions and the affect they have on you and how they drive and sometimes control you.

This realization came to me after having a conversation with a friend and realizing that I not only wanted this person to like me but ultimately to love me, too. I observed this need and for the first time. I questioned my motivation for this "needing to be loved." Who told me that someone is meant to love me? Do we spend our time looking for love or is there somebody out there who is just meant to love us?

I started questioning who I think should love me.

The first obvious candidates for the people who are meant to love me would be my parents. Aren't they meant to love me unconditionally? I think we all have stories of our parents not loving us in the ways we wanted, or not being there when we have needed them. Parents that have withdrawn or withheld their love, parents that have destroyed our trust, parents that were just too busy to be there, and parents who were not able to listen to or even hear us. Well, I will take them off the list of people who are meant to love me, as there seem to be too many conditions to their love. Don't get me wrong, I'm sure there are parents that have loved their kids unconditionally and accepted them the way they are, not wanted to influence them or persuade them to be the person they think they truly could be.

Then there is, of course, brothers and sisters. Surely they should love me because they are family, right? But then I became aware that they would rather play and hang out with somebody their own age like their own friends, or they would hang out with me because my parents made them, or they would hang out with me because they thought that's what a good sister or brother should do, not because they actually wanted to hang out. And there are always exceptions to this rule, but in my case, they are out.

And maybe it is my best friends; they will love me because that's what friends do, love me and be there for me. But they have other friends and sometimes they want to be with their other friends and not with me, or maybe they don't want to be with me all the time. So they are out as well.

So far in this life, nobody has been able to love me unconditionally all the time. Not my parents, not my brothers and sisters, not my best friends, so who is the person that is meant to be there for me and love me unconditionally? It is obviously none of these people so far. And if one of these people did love you, then now you are really convinced that someone is meant to love you.

Now in walks the concept of having a partner, a loved one, a soul mate. In romantic movies, this partner loves you, cares for you, never lets you down, is always by your side, is loyal, always loving and would do anything for you. And at the end of the movie, no matter much you have hurt each other, all is forgiven and you both live happily ever after. This is what I call the "Cinderella Syndrome." From a female perspective, some handsome prince comes along and takes you away from your life of struggle and unhappiness, takes you to a beautiful castle with unlimited wealth, loves you, and gives you everything you want, therefore you live happily ever after. For a male, you get the girl of your dreams. She loves you adoringly, is there for you to fulfill all your needs; she waits patiently for you while you go out to slay dragons, never complaining, and you live happily ever after. This is a false reality, a fairy tale that is not true. But how many people believe it to be true? I know not everyone has this story of what romantic love is, but it has been imprinted through our cultural and social conditioning for at least 200 years since the Brothers Grimm wrote their fairy tales.

Obtaining a loving partner seems to be the top goal of life for many people. The story sounds great: find a partner who loves and adores you, settle down, have children, and grow old together - the ultimate love story. But in reality, doesn't this seem to be one of the hardest things do and be successful at? Find the perfect unconditionally loving partner and then love them unconditionally? It can't be that easy, as the world seems to be full of single-parent families, marriage counselors, marriage guidance therapists, matrimonial settlement experts, and divorce lawyers.

Maybe the person that is meant to really love me is not a partner either? The idea of finding the perfect partner always seems very difficult, and I seem to have a lot of rules and expectations around how my partner should love me, even if I think I don't. I know why I have these rules. Mainly they are to keep me safe so no one can hurt me. So if it's not the partner that is meant to love me, then maybe it's my children? Maybe they are the ones to love me unconditionally? Hopefully, it is my children because I am running out of participants in the love game!

If I am a caring loving parent, then my children will see what a good parent I am and that I'm a good person, so they will love me. The only problem with children is that they seem to want to be loved unconditionally by you instead. So when you say to a child, "Come here, and I'll give you a hug," who really wants the hug? And you think the child doesn't know whom the hug is really for?

Now at this stage, I seem to have run out of options. Wait! Maybe it could be my work friends, but that's no good; some of them are always too busy. They don't necessarily want to hear what I'm doing. They seem to want to tell me about what they are doing. Perhaps if I am a good boss, my staff will respect and love me, but that doesn't seem to work either. Hey, this getting someone to love me unconditionally isn't that easy!

Now more questions start coming: *Maybe it's because I'm not a good person; that's why they don't love me? Or maybe I'm not lovable? Maybe I'm not likable? Maybe people think that I have nothing to say that is important? Maybe it's that I don't look perfect and they don't want to be seen with me? Or maybe I'm not intelligent enough, interesting enough, entertaining enough, funny enough, have enough money? Maybe it's because I'm fat? Maybe it's that I'm ugly? Maybe I don't have a very good personality?*

Maybe this is where all the big emotional stories in life come from when you don't get the love you want. Like, "You are not there for me," "I can't trust anybody; they will hurt me," "Nobody respects me," "I'm not good enough," "I don't fit in," "There's something wrong with me."

Maybe this is where the perceived negative feelings come from, like betrayal, or feeling disrespected or abandoned? Or the feeling of mistrust - that somebody is going to hurt you. I believe all these emotions and feelings come from a belief that somebody is meant to love you in your life, and these feeling arise when you don't get the love that you want and the love you think you should be getting from another person.

People could read this and want to fight me for their beliefs about getting love from another person as being the answer to happiness. They could say, "Aren't we all meant to experience love and feel love from another human being?" I truly believe that the purest feeling of love is when you give love to someone else without any of your own needs attached to it.

Now my questions turn to the beliefs: who told me that getting love from someone is the answer to my happiness? Who told me that this is true?

What if it is not true and no one is meant to love me, and that the only person who can really love me unconditionally is myself? But even this brings about a problem. How hard is it to love myself if I also have a belief that I'm not good enough? How can I love parts of myself that I don't like? How about the part that is judgmental of other people, or the part that likes to compare myself with others or competes with others to be better than them? Or the part that just sometimes doesn't care about anybody else? Or how about the part that is jealous of other people's lives, or the part that gets angry, or the part that is intolerant, or the part that is impatient, or the part that finds fault in others, or the part that thinks I'm better than others? These aren't all mine, but I have witnessed them in myself and others.

I think we all have stories like these and many others running in the background of our lives. When I think like this and catch myself having these thoughts, I wonder, where did they come from? What is my backstory or childhood experience that created these reactions? These stories on how I think life should be and definitely the story that I have created, believing that somebody is meant to love me?

What if all these emotions and feelings stem from just one single story, which is that I think that somebody is meant to love me, and having that will make me feel happy? Do you have this belief, too?

I think all of these thoughts and feelings come about when I think that I'm not getting the love I want. Maybe there is a link between all these feelings to the underlying story.

What if my "I'm not good enough" story is because I think I'm not good enough to be loved? What if "I judge others for doing things wrong" because I judge myself and because I think something is wrong with me and that no one will love me? What if "I compete with people and want to be better than them" is because if I'm better than others, people will look up to me and think I'm a good person and will love me more?

What if "I don't care about other people" is because I think they don't care about me, because if they did care about me then I would feel loved? What if "I'm jealous of people" because I think they are better, kinder, and more generous than I am so they will get more attention and love? Or what about "If I'm richer, people will think I am more successful and they will respect and love me more?" I could go on and on. Notice that all of these stories have a common theme running underneath them.

The realization I came to about the belief that "someone is meant to love me" is that it's *not true*. It's not true at all.

When I let go of that story, it was like a great weight lifted off my shoulders. I noticed my relationships with people changed. I no longer had expectations on them about how they should treat or be with me. How can you feel unloved if you don't need someone to love you? How can you feel betrayed if you don't need them to love you? How can you feel abandoned if you don't need them to love you? How can you feel disrespected if you don't need someone to love you? How can you feel unheard if you don't need someone to love you? How can you feel unseen if you don't need someone to love you? How can you feel lonely if you don't need someone to love you? And how can you feel that you're not good enough if you don't need someone to love you?

This one discovery has changed my life remarkably.

Now all I have to do is love myself for who I am unconditionally, that is, without conditions and judgments on my own performance and flaws. To accept that I'm not perfect and never can be, because what does perfect look like anyway? I accept that I make mistakes.

Not caring about how people see or perceive me and understanding my job in life isn't to keep people happy so they will like me, and not giving meaning to other people's opinions of me, it is just their opinion and their opinion comes through their filter of how they see the world, is incredibly liberating.

I am now free to be myself and enjoy growing and learning, doing the best I can and being okay with not doing the best I can. The only difference now is what is driving me. I'm not being driven by needing other people's approval and respect and love. I'm doing what I love. I'm living my life free from needing someone to love me. It's not that I don't give love and care to others freely and gladly; it's just that I don't need anything back from them to feel okay.

My affirmation is, "I refuse to give the power of how I feel to someone else."

Exercise 32.

Write your answers in your *Breaking Free* journal.

Title a new page: "The Greatest Deception Of Them All."

1. Who in your life do you think should love you?

2. If they love you, what should they do for you?

3. How would feel if you loved and accepted yourself completely?

4. What would it feel like if you had the freedom of not needing someone outside of yourself to love you?

5. I encourage you to look inside and ask yourself:

   a. Do I want people to love me?
   b. What do I feel when I don't get the love from others that I want?
   c. How do I react when I don't get the love that I want from others?

6. Imagine what it would feel like not to need anyone in the world to love you and that all you needed to do was to love yourself. How much space and freedom would there be for you around that? How happy and content would you be?

Chapter 34

What a Good Wife Should Do

I discovered recently that I had expectations about what I thought a wife should be like, how she should behave and what she should do for me. I also discovered that I had beliefs about what I should do as a husband, how I should behave and what I should do for my wife. Of course, the only problem with this is that my wife didn't know that I had these expectations and thoughts, let alone had we ever discussed them. The most frightening part of all was that I didn't know I had these expectations and ideas running in the background!

Now I understand why I would get upset with my wife when she didn't do the things the way I thought she should, as I had a set of rules for her to follow that she wasn't aware of. I personally think she should be able to read my mind, but she informs me she can't. We decided to do a process around this, which involved both of us writing down what our expectations were for each other. We used five different questions and decided not to compare or discuss the answers until we had both finished writing down our answers.

Try it for yourselves. You may be surprised what comes up for you and your partner. And if you don't have a partner, try it anyway. It may be very valuable for you to know your expectations before you enter into a relationship. You may want to re-evaluate what beliefs you take into your next relationship for your new partner's sake.

It turned out to be a very revealing and enlightening process not only with the answers to the questions but also the end effect it had on our relationship. Some of the things that came up for what I thought a good wife and mother should be were not unexpected, as I already knew I thought that way. The ones that surprised me were ideas I had running in the background that I didn't know existed. Where did they come from? I was truly unaware that I had these expectations for my wife - not only for her as my partner but also as a mother.

In reflection, some were old, entrenched views from my past relationships and from my childhood, and some I gained from watching my parents. Some of these views are totally outdated for this modern time.

I wasn't the only one with these hidden ideas and views, as my wife had her own set.

After discussing both of our lists and having some humor around our answers, we both gained a deeper understanding and respect for the other person's needs and beliefs. We spent time tracking back to the origins of these beliefs and questioning their validity and usefulness in our relationship.

Exercise 33.

Write your answers in your *Breaking Free* journal.

Title a new page: "What Should A Good Partner Do In A Relationship?

The five questions are:

1. What should a good partner do in a relationship?
2. What should a good husband do in a relationship?
3. What should a good father do in a relationship?
4. What should a good wife do in a relationship?
5. What should a good mother do in a relationship?

(Note: it doesn't matter if you don't have a husband or wife or whether you have children or not, answer all the five questions anyway.)

Summary

This process will uncover a whole realm of underlying beliefs and stories. Answering these questions proved to be a great way to strengthen our relationship and deepen our understanding of both ourselves and one another.

Stories About Money

Chapter 35

One Dollar a Week Can Change
Poverty Consciousness

The stories I had around money were tough to overcome and break free from. It seems to be an ongoing dilemma for many people other than myself. I have held deeply entrenched beliefs about money in my psyche. I was brought up with certain beliefs about money, how it works, what it's used for, how significant it is, how much time and effort is required to get it, and how important it is in life. I grew up listening to the views of other people about money, how schools, businesses, employers, councils, and governments perceive money and the importance placed on it. I observed the different affect it had on people and, most importantly, how it affects the happiness of people. I realize now that they are just beliefs and perceptions and are not necessarily true. The beliefs of the lower-income and higher-income earners can be different, but there are certainly similarities and threads that run through their thought patterns.

The capitalist system has created certain ideas about money, wealth, and how to attain them both. But man created the capitalist system, and it's not based on the laws of nature. Part of the capitalist system is built around loaning money and the interest earned on those loans. Some forms of loans are mortgages, credit cards, overdrafts, personal loans, car financing, hire purchase, and so on. As you can see, there are not too many people who haven't had one or more of these loans or mortgages and as such are paying interest in one form or another. So somebody is making money from us, as we have borrowed money from them to buy something. If you instead saved and accrued interest on your money and purchased items only when you could afford to, then the capitalist system would crumble, as all the big institutions would be paying you money and not the other way around. People don't usually live by what they can afford but by what they can borrow. I'm not saying everybody is like this. Seeing and understanding clearly about money and the monetary system is not necessarily an easy thing to do, especially if you have been fed misinformed ideas about money all your life like I have. Rich people don't have too many liabilities; they have assets. Assets earn them interest, so more money. It brings up a good question: Does the interest you receive outweigh the interest you are paying?

Money and financial systems have their own language, which is difficult to comprehend at the best of times even by people who deal with money; banks don't even necessarily understand and comprehend its complexities. A great example of this was the 2008 financial collapse. How come so many financial institutions didn't see it coming, and even when it was happening, the banks refused to admit it. On a side note, there is a great movie, *The Big Short*, which is based on a true story and sheds light on what happened in the 2008 financial crash. Even though they explained it well in the movie, the financial crash and the events leading up to it were still a bit difficult to understand. Well, it was for me!

Many very wealthy and successful business people have shared the commonly held concept of saving 10%, giving away 10%, and living off the rest for years. I first became aware of it in a book called *Rich Dad Poor Dad* by Robert T. Kiyosaki and Sharon Lechter. If I had been told and had understood this knowledge when I was 20 years old, I would be an awfully rich man by now. Instead, I bought into part of the poverty consciousness of saving money, then spending the money I'd saved on something I wanted, becoming poor again, and then saving again until I had enough to buy something else, allowing the cycle to continue. I believe poverty consciousness sounds like this: "There is never enough, and we always need more than what we have."

For the last ten years, my friend Ray has been telling me how to break this cycle. This is no exaggeration. I never "heard" him. For ten years, he kept telling me, and for ten years, I couldn't hear him. I mean, I heard what he had to say. I just didn't understand what he was saying. So this knowledge I will give to you and hope you don't take ten years to hear it like I did. It's really simple.

Here it goes: Save 10% of all your income. But don't save this money with plans to spend it. No, this is the money you save with absolutely no intention of ever spending. I will say this again, so you can hear: Save this money and never spend it. Make it work for you and make interest from it, but never spend it. Even to the day you die. Instead, leave it as a legacy to your children and teach them the financial principle that comes with never spending it. This is something most wealthy people do because they understand the principle. Keep adding to it in your life and pass it on to your children. And if you want to save money to buy something, use a different account.

I know there are people and cultures that already teach this to their children. These are the people we see and say, "Look at that rich guy; he's so lucky. He inherited old family money. That's why he's so rich." Exactly. Imagine if your great-great-grandfather saved 10% of his earnings his whole life and invested it in things that made him more money, didn't spend any of it, and lived on the remaining 90%. And imagine if your grandfather did this as well and taught your mother or father to do this. How much wealth do you think would have been accumulated throughout these generations?

What have you been born into where money is concerned? What are your family beliefs around money? What are your mother's beliefs? What are your father's beliefs? How have they impacted on you?

Now, for what I believe is the most important aspect of this 10% saving account, and it has very little to do with the money: How it makes you feel. This is no great secret. Putting money away each week and having no intention of ever spending it changes the way you think about money, and that is the key.

It's not about the money. It's about having money earn you money, and how that makes you feel. It's how it affects your mindset around money. It's that simple. I suggest you don't let your mind try and understand this but instead just do it. You have nothing to lose; even one dollar a week is enough. The main reason for this account is the psychological effect it has on you - about you feeling rich.

The key is that you need to put one dollar or more away each and every week. Don't miss a week even if it is only a dollar. Don't say to yourself, "I will catch up next week and put in two dollars." It won't work that way. What you are really saying is you don't have enough to put in this week, and the message you are giving out is that you don't have enough. So that is what will happen: you won't ever have enough. Or if the story is, "I didn't have time to put it in this week," then your story will be that you never have enough time to make money.

So the main principle of having this account is that it constantly reminds you that you are getting richer every week. You are constantly earning interest on your money and you are constantly getting richer every day. It has to be done each week so your mind knows that each week you are saving money and accumulating more wealth and abundance. Remember the primary goal of this saving 10% of your income exercise is to transform the relationship you have with money. It's as simple as that. You then get the privilege of setting your children and your children's children free from poverty consciousness and instead you get to teach them about prosperity. It's got to start sometime, so you might as well be the one to start it off.

At this stage, I must mention another important principle in the attraction of financial wealth and abundance. That is the principle of tithing. Saving money and tithing are two of the most important principles in gaining financial freedom. It is interesting that both of these two things are about changing the way you see and think about money. Tithing honors the principle of generosity and abundance in the Law of Attraction. If you are generous to other people, then other people will be generous to you, and money will come to you in unexpected ways. Generosity breeds generosity; it is just that simple.

Tithing isn't about just giving to the poor or the needy. It could be giving money to a trust or society or group of people who are trying to make a difference in the world. It is a known fact that many very wealthy people tithe to their favorite charity, aid groups, or organizations. It is the principal of the tithing that is the most important thing because it changes your mind and belief structure. This is one of the key principles in the Law of Attraction and is a very well documented and proven concept. Generosity grows your heart and your kindness, which influences your character and the way you see the world, while also directly influencing your personal relationship with money. Changing the way you see money is one of the major aspects of how to become truly free.

Exercise 34.

Write your answers in your *Breaking Free* journal.

Title a new page: "I Grow My Financial Abundance And Wealth Every Day."

1. Set a goal that within four days, you will have opened an account and you will be directly depositing a minimum of $1 a week, or up to 10% of your income each week into this account for the rest of your life on this planet, knowing that you will never spend it.

2. Find a group or charity that you support and make weekly or monthly donations to this organization. Observe how your generosity filters back to you in other ways. This is a simple principle of abundance.

Summary

See if your stories around money and your mind will try and talk you out of believing it can be this easy. You may find your mind will try and talk you out of doing either of these two tasks. That's how strong our belief stories can be. If you can override the way your mind thinks and complete these two tasks, then they will change the way you believe and see money, wealth, and abundance forever.

If you have started this account and set up the donations by the time you finish this book, your prosperity has already started.

Chapter 36

Save One Dollar A Week,
Or The Money Tree Theory

The $1 or 10% a week you save and put away should only be spent on ways of making more money, like interest-bearing accounts, earning money with your money and compound interest accounts. When you have enough, you can buy an investment, which will make you more money. The secret to this account mentioned in the last chapter is that you never spend any of the money that you have saved; you keep growing it forever. The money needs to keep moving and growing or it will stagnate. Eventually, you will be able to live off the money it generates, but you need seed money first. Let me explain what I mean by seed money.

The Money Tree Theory

You need to plant a seed to grow a tree, so it can grow and produce fruit. Then you can live off the fruits of the tree; otherwise, you can keep eating the seeds and never grow any trees that generate fruit. This is the same principle of growing money. You need to invest money to make it grow, or you will just keep spending it and won't have fruit from your savings, just seeds. The more you water and fertilize the tree, the faster and more it grows, and the more fruit you get. Like in nature, the fruit keeps growing while you are asleep - growing in value, quality, and size. You will always want to keep the tree and never chop it down. Or just like the popular golden goose idiom: you should always keep the goose that lays the golden eggs. If you eat the goose for dinner, you will never get any more eggs.

The tree will eventually produce enough fruit to live on, which is the principle of any investment: to create enough interest to live on without touching your principal investment, or until you can buy a different cash generator to create more money to live on, or until you can plant more trees. Also, remember you don't have to have just one tree or one goose; you can have as many as you like. You can have an entire orchard or a geese farm. It's up to you. I might go for the orchard. It's a lot quieter. However, the principle of compounding wealth is still the same.

Exercise 35.

> 1. Have you planted your first seed yet through opening an account and depositing your first dollar?
>
> 2. Have you donated money to your favorite charity or set up a monthly direct payment?

Summary

I encourage you to do these two things - depositing a dollar, or 10%, into an account each week and tithing - as these two vital steps are the first in the creation of financial freedom. If you have, you will already be creating interest on it, which means you have already made money. Don't wait ten years like I did. I don't want to even imagine how much fruit I would have had by now if I had listened. Thank goodness Ray never gave up on me. He told me about the principles of wealth and money. It gave me the opportunity to change the way I view money, even if I was a bit slow with the uptake.

The money story is just another story we have been taught. Breaking free from this story will change your wealth, financial abundance, the way you see money and prosperity, and will change your bank balance.

How To Break
The Stories

Chapter 37

How To Change Feeling Negativity

Focus on the positive. That phrase is only four very simple words - easy to say, yet not always easy to do. Sometimes it is very hard to get out of a negative state. It's as if the negativity consumes you. When I get into this negative space, it's comfortable. I know it well. It's familiar to me. Even though it's not a so-called "nice" feeling, I am content staying in this feeling and wallowing in my misery. It's a familiar pattern and a story that I can slip into. I've talked about the Law of Attraction, which is: whatever you focus on amplifies. In Chinese Medicine, it is said, "Where the mind goes, the Qi or energy goes." So if I focus on a negative feeling, it will create more negative feelings.

A great teaching, but did I want to apply this? No! I wanted to mourn a bit longer. I didn't want to let go of the feeling or witness my attachment to a negative way of thinking. I wanted to talk more about what I was experiencing in order to justify and strengthen my stories. I realized that to change this emotional state, I needed to change my focus. And not just to focus on the positive, but to take action. Only focusing on what I wanted to happen wasn't going to be enough. I needed to stand up, move around, and go somewhere different. I needed to grow a stronger, compelling story, a story that was more powerful than the old negative story, which was destroying and hurting me. These stories were self-destructive and had too much control over me.

So how do I override the old stories and grow more constructive, positive and powerful stories?

Tony Robbins has a three-step process to change a negative mindset. He says to:

1. Change your physiology.

Sit up, shoulders back, and chest out. Do this while you are reading this and you will be able to feel a difference straight away. Stand up, stand on one leg, hop around like a rabbit, or walk like a chicken. Just change the way you were physically before and do something different. You might find your mind fighting with you, saying things like, "That won't make a difference," or "That's stupid," or "It can't be that easy," "I don't want to," "I can't be bothered with that," or "What a waste of time."

Or you could choose to ignore your mind chatter and negative self-talk and simply stand up and walk around like a chicken to see if it works. I don't mean walk like an unhappy chicken either. I mean walk like a rooster, king of the coup or queen of the coup, depending on the gender of your chicken. Tell me that after doing this, you didn't start smiling and feeling different? Of course, you can do anything to change your physiology: jump up and down, dance, spin around, and do anything to break the state and body language you are in. The wilder and stranger, the better. Get right out of your comfort zone. This may not be easy, as all of your stories will try to stop you. But who is in control? You or the depressed person? Take the control back and stand up!

2. Change your language.

Transform negative complaining into positive commenting. It's not a complaint if you bring the issue that you have to the person who can change it; you can state facts or opinions without a complaining tone.

Practice positive comments. Use words such as "fantastic, outstanding, wonderful, magnificent, brilliant, spectacular, stunning, impressive, amazing, adorable, courageous, fearless, brave, beautiful, valiant, lovable." Create your own list of words that inspire you. Write positive affirmations and find a few positive comments or verses on the topic that you have a negative story around and that you may have found yourself stuck in. As an example, for me, it is around money and paying the bills. Now I say, "I always have financial abundance," "I can always pay my bills on time," "I always have enough money to pay my bills," and "I always have plenty of money left over." The great thing about this is if you go on Google and type in "positive affirmations related to the statement, 'I don't think I am good enough,'" you will find pages and pages of examples stating why you are good enough.

List the negative stories you have and pick a positive affirmation to override them. Say them every day for the rest of your life and every day will be a good day. Pick the ones you like. These are the bullets for your gun to wage war and defeat the enemy of negative feelings and negative stories.

If you are competitive then see it as a game. You play to win; winning feels great and losing sucks. Use the positive words to defeat the negative words, stories, and feelings. Ask yourself, "Do I want to be a loser or do I want to be a winner?" Refuse to lose, stand up, and fight! Ha, that sounds like a motivational talk before the World Cup Rugby final. Could you imagine the coach of the team standing up before the game and saying, "Okay guys, we are useless, we are going to lose, we are hopeless, it's a waste of time trying, nobody likes you, so go out and have a great game." You overcome the odds with greatness and not negativity.

3. Change your focus.

Don't look at what is wrong; look for what is right. Focus on the great things in your life. Focus on the excitement and adventure, the joy and happiness. Harness the feelings that come with focusing on the positive to defeat the negative. Read inspiring books, watch inspiring movies and documentaries or Ted Talks, and surround yourself with uplifting people. Focus on everything that is right in the world. Look at the flowers, not the weeds. Look at the blue sky, not the clouds. Focus on the half-full glass, not the glass half empty.

If you use these three simple steps every time you notice that you're stuck in a negative emotional state, it will be almost impossible to stay there. Then keep affirming and growing the positivity every day, morning, noon, and night, and your experience of life will completely transform. I forgot this and got caught in one of my old stories, but not again. I'm a winner!

Exercise 36.

Write your answers in your *Breaking Free* journal.

Title a new page: "Positive Affirmations."

1. Write down 5 positive affirmations on how you want your life to be.

   Some examples of affirmations are:
   a. Gratitude is in my heart and soul and is in every cell of my body.
   b. I like creating positive compelling stories around how I see others and myself.
   c. I am living a long, happy, and healthy life.

   I challenge you to repeat your five affirmations once every morning and once at night for the next 21 days. Notice how you feel after you say them each day.

2. Create a section in your *Breaking Free* journal and title it "The 21-Day Challenge." Number each day and write down how you felt on that day for the next 21 days.

3. On day 7, 14 and 21 write down what changes have occurred in your life since starting the 21-day challenge and declare your five affirmations twice a day.

Summary

By saying positive affirmations every day, it will keep your mind and heart in a positive place. It will help you look at the light, not the shadows. It will help you to see things in a positive way and help you to see what is right with the world instead of only what is wrong.

Chapter 38

Make Feeling Happy Easy

Earlier in my life I had a tendency to set my goals too high, and the closer I got to them, the further I would move them away. I think the official term is "moving the goal post." An example for me was buying a house with a mortgage with the goal of owning my own home someday. As I paid it off and had more equity in the house, I would re-mortgage it to pay for an extension and alterations and thus put myself into more debt. Then before paying it off, I would sell it and buy a bigger, newer, more stylish house and put myself into even more debt. This is an example of moving the goal post for me. I was always looking into the far-off future to achieve my first existing goal, which was to own my own home. I made it ever increasingly harder to achieve this goal. I'm not saying not to invest in your asset. I'm encouraging you to make the goals easier or smaller. In this case, maybe the goal may have been to build an extension and sell the house and make a 10% profit. Then I would have felt happy about achieving the goal instead of having the goal 30 to 40 years out in the future. Remember, this is my story. Many people have shorter-term goals around their real-estate dealings.

It's not that I think setting goals and aspiring to grow and expand is not a great thing. It's that I had a tendency to want to move the "goal post" after I got close to the goal. The concern I have with changing the goal post is that if I associate my level of happiness, success, and contentment with the success of reaching my goals, then I was creating a situation where feeling happy was going to be very hard to achieve. I was consistently changing the finish line. So I asked myself the obvious question, "Why did I want to do this to myself"?

I found there was a myriad of underlying stories and reasons behind it. I had stories like "Life can't be that easy" and "If I achieve my goals then what in life is left to achieve?" or "If I reach my goals, I will have nothing to do," "No pain, no gain," "You can never 'rest on your laurels,'" "You can always do better," and the big one: "If I have a bigger, flashier house, people will think I'm more successful." Some of these things comments are positives in themselves, but not when they are associated with achieving goals.

Once I realized I was moving the goal posts, I decided to make my goals easier to achieve and to then savor the feelings of success, which achieving my goals provided. The theory of the Law of Attraction is the more you feel something, the more you will attract that into your life. I decided to embrace the feelings that came with achievement, and I would sit in this space and bask in the feelings of completion. I would make feeling happier and contentment easier to achieve. This seems much better than having a goal of happiness and contentment so far away that I made it nearly impossible to reach. And in my case, to move the goals further away every time I got close, which made it even more difficult to experience feelings of success.

It's like having the goal of winning the lottery. I have heard myself and others say, "If I win the lottery, then all my problems will go away, I will be happy, and I won't have to worry about anything ever again." What is the chance of winning the Lotto? It's a one in 3.8 million chance of winning the first division in the New Zealand lottery. So the reality is, I will most probably never win the lotto. Does this mean I will always have problems? That I will always be worrying about things and never be happy? Because that's what I'm saying if I don't win the Lotto. I don't think this is a very good goal to pin my longing for happiness on. I might be waiting a long time and in this case forever. I think achieving goals is just one of many ways to experience feelings of happiness. I have goals of owning a M3 BMW, owning my dream house, and having an occupation where I make $500,000 a year. All of these would also make me happy, but I may want to bring the goals a bit closer to home so I can practice the feeling, and the truth is, by doing that, the bigger goals may come a little quicker. I also think there are ways to feel happiness that are a little easier to achieve as well as something I can aspire to every day. Of course, I'm not saying don't aspire to the big things too, but why not?

So now I grow the feeling of achieving every day. I feel happy when I wake up in the morning and it's a new day, and then I feel even happier when I look over and see my lovely wife and best friend beside me. I feel happy walking to the park to do my Taiji and Qigong practice in the morning. I feel happy to have a shave and a shower to wash away the night's sleep and freshen myself up for the new day. I feel happy to put on clean clothes. I feel happy to have a delicious breakfast, and I feel happy to get ready to greet the first person I meet in my new exciting day. Happiness doesn't have to be hard to achieve. It's a state of mind and heart that requires making a choice.

Exercise 37.

Write your answers in your *Breaking Free* journal.

Title a new page: "I Feel Happy And Grateful Every Day Of My Life."

1. Write down 5 things that make you happy.

2. Write down 5 things that you are grateful for.

Summary

Making happiness easier to achieve seems to be a great way to spend my day. Even if something happens in my day that is unexpected and difficult, I can still choose to see it as an opportunity to learn and grow. I'm not saying that I have this completely sorted out all of the time, but I am practicing and aspiring to be like this every day. Life in this world seems too short to be discontent, unfulfilled, and dissatisfied. Pick happiness; it's simply a choice.

Chapter 39

How To Get Back The Feeling Of Happiness And Excitement In Your Life

I was observing a group of children playing, noticing how happy they were, and I wondered: *When did I lose that youthful happiness?* Not that I'm not a positive person now, but when did I lose that childhood joy? I remember when I used to drink alcohol, which gave me a feeling of youthful exuberance. I wondered why I needed to get intoxicated to get it back and why I couldn't access this feeling without it.

Do all the stresses and responsibilities of being an adult take it away? The responsibility of having a job, paying bills, buying things you need, cooking for others, paying the rent or a mortgage, running the house, expenses such as life insurance, medical insurance, doctors, dentists, taxes, superannuation, investments, owning and running transport such as cars, motorbikes, and boats, relationships, partnerships, children, social engagements, sex, the list goes on. I'm getting tired and stressed just thinking about it! What about keeping fit and healthy, maintaining your appearance, or buying clothes and entertainment?

It seems that all a child has to think about is having fun, playing, eating food, and sleeping. That doesn't sound at all stressful to me. I noticed children do not think too far into the future either. They can stay present to the situation that they are in. They don't seem to have a lot of worries either until we start giving them some, like when we tell them, "No, don't do that," "Don't touch that," "You will hurt yourself," "Don't be so silly," "What will people think of you if they see you doing that?" (This one might not necessarily be about the child.)

What about the line, "You have to get a good education to get a good job so you can make more money and have a better lifestyle." Does your child really know what that means anyway? They are just words to a child. What about, "Eat your vegetables and you will grow up to be big and strong." What does that mean to a 10-year-old? They may ask, "Why do we need to be big and strong?" They have no real term of reference or understanding of what you are really saying. What does "grow up to be strong" mean? Is strong something we get when we are older? What age does that happen? The most ironic part of the statement is that in most cases the young child is more fit and strong for their size than their parents.

The messages I would like to think that we are giving our children are to help them understand life and prepare them for later when some of the childhood freedoms seem to stop and the need to create income and responsibilities start. That sounds very depressing when I say is like that. It doesn't sound much fun for a child to look forward too either. As an adult, wouldn't it be fun not to have all the responsibilities and just get up in the morning and do anything you want, eat whatever you felt like, hang out with whomever you wanted to? Wouldn't it be great to do things because you wanted to, not because you felt you had to? This is an interesting form of freedom.

Losing the joy and happiness seems to come from doing things we don't really want to do. I have talked to many of my clients over the years and many are not happy with their occupations. They do it for the money, which they use to survive. Children don't necessarily understand the concept of needing money to survive and generally don't have this issue with money. When they want money, they ask their parents (not that they always get it, of course).

I noticed I used to get angry with my son when he had left school for just lying in bed or relaxing in front of the TV when I was going to work, but the truth for me is that I just wanted to do the same or at least I wanted the freedom to do it.

One of the ways I broke free and discovered joy and happiness again in my life was that I wrote down all the things that made me happy on a list. This is similar to one of my other favorite lists, the "Things I Love to Do" list.

These lists have to be one of the most useful tools I have found in discovering happiness. It is simple but most profound. All you need to do is write a list of all the things that make you happy. (This is in the *Breaking Free* journal exercise below.) It may take some time and thought. Things will come to you for days after you have started this process. Just start writing down things that make you happy in a list. Start with ten items, but don't stop at ten; keep going. If you aren't at home, it may be helpful to carry around a notepad and pen so you can write down your ideas as they come to you or you could keep a list on your phone. So that you don't forget them later, add them to your big list when you get home. Write down all the things you think of, no matter how small. For example, a couple of mine are that I feel happy when I'm eating peanut butter and banana on toast, and I feel happy having a hot shower. Write down physical experiences you might feel happy when you are dancing, running, walking in nature, or skydiving. Something I love and makes me feel happy is the physical feeling of acceleration. Unfortunately, traffic officers don't seem to understand this fascination!

One of the keys to this process is to say to yourself whilst enjoying what makes you happy is, "I love doing this; it makes me happy." Saying this will bring your attention to the feeling. I feel happy riding my motorbike, so when I am riding it I say to myself, "I feel happy right now riding my bike," and I smile all the way to where I'm going and all the way back. Try it. It works. Write down the things that make you happy like the time of day that makes you happy, the season of the year, food, animals, colors, flavors, scents, restaurants, music, artists, authors, movies, etc.

I have a friend who wrote "dancing" on her list and she hadn't danced for years. When she identified that she really loved to dance, she started attending dance classes and now she goes out dancing. It made me smile too, as I can see her dancing with a smile on her face and feeling joy again in her life.

An important point is that if things that do *not* make you happy come up when you are writing your list, as they seem to do, don't write them down or give them any attention.

Let the "Things That Make Me Happy" list have a lot of time to expand. Write down the things that would make you happy but that you haven't done yet as well.

Lastly, once you have written the list, start doing the things on that list, whether you have been doing them already or not. Enjoy the things that make you happy.

Exercise 38.

Write your answers in your *Breaking Free* journal.

Title a new page: "What Makes Me Happy And Free."

> 1. What makes you happy? Write a list of ten things that makes you happy and then start doing all of them today.

> 2. What do you do that makes you feel free from everything? Do that daily.

Summary

So now I am learning to play again, to do the things that make me happy, to do things that make me laugh, and to live more with the feeling of freedom I had as a child. I have more adventures and I search for new experiences. I "boldly go where no man has gone before," just like the *Star Trek* quote. Didn't we all enjoy watching *Star Trek* and want to have amazing adventures in outer space, or was that just me?

If you're looking for me in the summertime, I'm the one building sandcastles at the beach and sitting inside the sandcastle trying to stop the waves coming over the moat. I will feel like I have no responsibilities or worries in the world - well, except for a large wave coming.

Start To See Life
A New Way

Chapter 40

The Pure Essence of Our Souls

Take away the mind chatter; take away the stories from our childhood; take away our views on religion and politics; take away our opinions about global warming; take away our ideas of our monetary values and the capitalist system; take away our ideas on what success looks like, our views on what a good relationship or good parenting looks like, and what do you have left? Who are you without all of these thoughts and opinions? Who are you without your busy mind? Who are you when your mind is quiet?

Who are you without your mind's ideas, views, opinions, beliefs, and stories? What is left in the stillness? I believe it is you. You as your pure self, you without your mind to distract you. You in the essence of your heart and you in your purity. You without stories that don't serve you. You without memories of your parents not listening or understanding you. You without the feelings and memories of being alone. You without any expectation that you have to be somebody. You without the expectation that you should be good, study hard, get a good job, work hard, get married, buy a house, and live happily ever after.

Have you ever wondered who said this is the way we should live or the way we should think? Who made up this way of existence? I want to challenge this way of living and this way of thinking. I want to challenge this way of living my life. I believe there is another way to see the world, a world away from our minds and our thoughts. A world free from your points of views and opinions. I think it is the world that is seen through your heart, not your mind. I believe your heart sees life very differently than your mind.

Let me explain. Here is an exercise to show you the difference. Put your index and middle finger on your forehead and then think of a person you don't necessarily like and what is it that you don't like about them. As you continue thinking of them, think of more things you don't like about them. If you don't know of anybody you don't like or anybody that annoys you, then make somebody up. I'm sure you can find somebody. As you think of them, become the silent witness of your own mind and notice how busy it is with lots of negative thoughts and opinions. Now put your hands on your heart and think of the same person through your heart. How do you see them? I would be surprised if you don't see them differently. You can see how they are struggling and how they are doing the best they possibly can under their own personal struggles and circumstances. You may even get an insight into why they do what they do. I have done this exercise many times with myself and other people, and every time the person has seen the person they were thinking about completely differently from their heart. Your heart sees people with compassion and kindness. It sees their unhappiness and struggles, and it sees the real person without their stories.

My point is, if you can see people differently from your heart rather than your head, then I bet you will be able to see life differently too. Generally, your heart doesn't have judgment; it has a clear vision, understanding, and compassion. It doesn't react to the person's comments but instead tries to understand the other's individual point of view and sometimes their pain.

Another example of this is next time you feel put down, angry or frustrated, and you feel like retaliating, ask yourself, who is the person I'm wanting to defend? Who am I trying to protect from experiencing feelings of rejection, pain, or shame? Is this person in your head, or in your heart? Who was the little child that felt alone? When you think of this lonely little child, does he or she live in your head or your heart?

These concepts are sometimes hard to understand and experience as your mind constantly tries to make some sense and understanding. The thing to remember is that it isn't a mind experience; it is a heart experience, and our minds will constantly try to take control and be in charge. It will even try to convince you that you can't look at life through your heart as the mind doesn't want to lose control.

Here is another example: think of somebody who you love, put both your hands on your forehead, and say out loud, "I love such and such." Go on try it. Now put both hands on your heart and say the same thing, "I love such and such." Notice the difference in the quality of feelings that you experience. From your head, it seems like a statement. From your heart, it's more like a feeling and an emotional experience.

I encourage you to practice looking and living life through your heart. When you do this, it's a very different world. And if you already do live through your heart, keep on spreading this understanding to the world. It is a practice, but your mind won't give up without a fight. It will constantly try to bring you back into your stories, judgments, and opinions. We have opinions about everything, opinions about situations, and opinions about people. Only the heart can break free from these.

Exercise 39.

Write your answers in your *Breaking Free* journal.

Title a new page: "Thinking From My Heart."

1. Write down what you have discovered through your experience of thinking from your head.

2. Write down what you have discovered through your experience of thinking from your heart.

3. Write down any observations you had while thinking from these two different centers.

Summary

My encouragement is to have a go at living in a world without your opinions, beliefs, and points of view. Just observe the world with wonderment and a sense of adventure. See nature and its beauty with amazement. See all the opportunities and choices in life. See people from the wisdom of understanding and not from judgment. See from your heart and you'll be able to see the truth.

Chapter 41

Say How You Feel

Saying how you are feeling can be difficult sometimes, especially if you don't know how you are really feeling. There are many spiritual and emotional practices that involve sensing into how you are feeling. Try this for yourself right now. Just sit and feel into your body, and ask yourself: "How am I feeling, and what do I feel in my body?"

For example, you may be feeling tired, hungry, happy, or frustrated. Your mind may be racing. You may feel cold or hot. You may feel pain in your lower back. You may feel the pressure of your bottom if you are sitting. You may feel warm or cold hands or feet. As you read this chapter, stay aware of your body. This is a practice - to be engaged in some activity while also maintaining awareness of your body and how you are feeling at the same time. Men may find this more difficult to do than women, but it is sometimes not easy for either to do.

People meditate for years to be able to feel into themselves. This may sound a bit strange, but you know what I mean. One part is being *aware* of how you are feeling, and the second part of being able to *explain* what the feeling is. This can be challenging for some and easy for others. It would be like explaining what snow feels like to a person who has lived their life in the tropical climate of Singapore. How do you put the feeling of cold into words when it's an experience of the body, not the mind?

I imagine that most of us probably spend much of our time in our minds, not sensing into the feelings in our bodies. I love it when people ask me, "How are you?" and I say most of the time "Fine, thanks," "Great, thanks," or similar responses. These comments seem like such an empty answer. Now sometimes I might say, and this depends on who asks, "Well, my old shoulder injury is playing up today; my tinnitus is as loud as ever; my eyesight is getting worse; my hair is getting grey and falling out; my wife and I are getting on great; my mother passed away recently; I love my car - it is running well, and I love driving it; work is busy and I've had lots of interesting new patients this week; I've been feeling a bit down today after my mum's passing and a bit tired as I have been working a lot of late nights on my new website - wait 'til you see it! Thanks for asking. How are you doing?"

This is a very similar answer to what I got when I asked a friend in Malaysia, "How are you?" He told me about himself in great detail because in their culture if you ask that question, they think you really want to know, whereas in other countries, in my opinion, it is more of a greeting with the understanding that people really don't want to know everything that's going on with you or how you're feeling. But this is not always true, as sometimes people really do want to know how you are.

What I'm really pointing at is that, if somebody asked you how you are feeling, do you feel into yourself and give them the truth? Do you say things like, "I'm feeling [happy, content, angry, worried, excited] today," or "I'm not enjoying my new job; I feel like it's not what I really want to do," or I'm struggling with one of my friends at the moment," or "I'm feeling tired and pissed off and bored with my life and my job" - or whatever is true for you at the time?

I now attempt to feel more into myself and speak about how I'm really feeling to those who really ask. I also try to interpret my state of mind as well as my emotions and physical body states. There seems to be a freedom that comes with really acknowledging how I am feeling. It has deepened my understanding of myself and my relationship with others.

Exercise 40.

Write your answers in your *Breaking Free* journal.

Title a new page: "How Do I Really Feel Today?"

1. Sit and feel into your body for five minutes and then write down exactly how you are feeling.

2. Next time someone asks you how you are feeling, tell them but use your discretion with how much you say. It's more important that you are aware of how you are feeling than it is telling everyone.

Summary

I think it is a real treasure to be able to feel into yourself and say how you are feeling, but it does take practice. In a situation of anger, be aware if the person who asks you how you are feeling is not the one that you are angry with. You may want to decide beforehand whether it would be constructive and beneficial to tell them or not.

I remember the words that were told to me one day by one of my teachers. He said, "Say what you mean, mean what you say, or say nothing at all because sometimes it serves no purpose or value to the other person to say what you really think." These are very wise words. So, ask me next time you see me how I am feeling. I may get you a chair and sit down with you and tell you.

Chapter 42

Be True To Your Word

I have often heard the saying, "Be true to your word," and I have discovered there is a deeper meaning behind these words that I want to share. But first, let's look at the basic meaning and understanding of these words: "Be honest with what you say." If you say something, then you will keep your word and do it. It's generally about keeping one's promise.

In the reality of this world, quite often this does not happen for various reasons and has become common practice for people to say things that could be untrue.

I believe that most people generally try to do the right thing, yet many good people lie frequently or say untruths as part of their day-to-day lives. I'm definitely not saying that everybody does this, but these white lie or untruths have become commonplace. How often, for example, have we told untruths in order to get out of social engagements like, "I'd love to come, but I'm busy that night," or "I'm sorry, I've got something else going on at that time."

How often have we said untruths, or asked our children or co-workers to say untruths on our behalf, like when you get a phone call from someone you don't want to talk to: "Tell them I'm not here!" or if you do answer, "I'd love to chat, but I'm late for a meeting," or "I'd love to chat, but I've got to get this job finished."

How many couples regularly say untruths to each other for fear of hurting each other's feelings or getting into a conflict, such as "I'm not mad, I'm just upset about work," or "I'll be home in ten minutes," or "I'm not upset, I'm just tired."

How often do we lie to ourselves: "Tomorrow I'll go to the gym," or "I'll pay off that credit card next month."

We may think that saying these untruths is for a good reason: to keep from upsetting or wounding someone we love, to avoid our own discomfort of being a failure, out of our own integrity, to smooth over conflict, or to make someone happy. We may even think it will help us to avoid the pain of disappointing someone, of facing a difficult truth or of being the bearer of bad news.

I believe that by saying these untruths there can be a more devastating consequence. By understanding the Law of Attraction, the belief that by focusing on positive or negative thoughts you can bring positive or negative experiences, you may well bring these untruths into reality. I have seen this happen.

In the book, *The Four Agreements* by author and Toltec wise man, Don Miguel Ruiz, Ruiz presents a simple but profound code of personal conduct based on adhering to four basic principles or "agreements." The very first agreement is, "Be impeccable with your word." In explaining this agreement, he says, "Speak with integrity. Say only what you mean. Avoid using the word to speak against yourself or to gossip about others. Use the power of your word in the direction of truth and love."

I believe the spoken word has consequences and these words have more power and affect than we realize.

If you say you're going to be somewhere at 7 p.m. and you arrive at 7.15 p.m., then the message you are sending out into the universe is that you don't keep your word, and if you don't keep your word, then the Law of Attraction won't keep its word. This is the dynamic you are creating. So if you ask for something and you aren't true to your word, the Law of Attraction might not be true to its word either, and you won't get what you ask for.

It's common sense how this would work - energy attracts energy, positive attracts positive, suffering attracts more suffering. If you think life is easy and everything works out for the best all the time, then that is what will happen. But if you think life is a struggle and is hard, then life will be a struggle and it will be hard. I have seen this simple truth played out in so many peoples lives including my own.

Here is a simple guide to help you attract positive events into your life:

- If you say you are going to do something, then make sure you follow through on it.
- Always keep your promises, and if you know you cannot, then don't make them. If you cannot keep your promise to remain in integrity and being true to yourself, then honor that too. It could also be because sometimes you make a promise and it works out that it is impossible to keep; sometimes circumstances are beyond your control. Be

okay with that as well. All you can only ever do is your best at the time.

- When you give your word that you are going to do something, your word has to be your bond.
- Learn not to make promises you don't intend to keep, and certainly don't pledge yourself to something you can't follow through on.

In short:

- If you give your word to another, stick to it.
- If you make a promise to another, abide by it.
- If you say you are going to do something, do it.
- And lastly, remember you are not perfect and you can make mistakes and misjudgments. Honor your good intentions, honor your humanness, and grow your honesty.

Exercise 41.

Write your answers in your *Breaking Free* journal.

Title a new page: "Be True To Your Word."

1. Now that you are aware that you might possibly say untruths, I encourage you to write down in your *Breaking Free* journal what you say every time you catch yourself saying something that might not really be true.

2. Write down any times that you may already be aware of when you haven't spoken the truth.

235

3. Write down each time you say something and you don't do exactly what you said you were going to do.

Summary

My Taiji master once said to me that I try to live by: "Say what you mean, mean what you say, or say nothing at all."

Another great saying to live by is by Gautama Buddha: "If you propose to speak, always ask yourself, is it true, is it necessary, is it kind?"

Speaking the truth is about being true to yourself and what you could attract into your life if you don't. The Law of Attraction will keep its side of the contract; all you have to do is keep yours.

Chapter 43

The Big Five

I was teaching a Qigong class that morphed into a philosophy lesson, and I believe we uncovered the five biggest stories that run in the background and control most of our lives. It started when somebody in class asked, "How do you know what stories are affecting our lives?" I felt into the question and realized that the best way to discover and understand the source of the stories was to have a physical experience of the answer. So firstly we practiced a few Qigong exercises to get everyone into their hearts and out of their heads.

How I started this process was by getting the people in the class to move around the room, shaking each other's hands. As they shook the hand of the other person, I asked them to think to themselves what the person was like and to keep what they thought private. Then I got everyone to put their left hand on their hearts and shake hands with everyone, this time thinking from their hearts what the other person was like. I asked them to compare the different impressions they got. Almost everyone saw the person differently when they looked at the people from their hearts than from their heads.

I invited people to shake each other's hands with the intention of wanting the other person to like them, but not saying anything to them. People smiled and laughed as they shook hands. When we stopped, they shared how it felt. Some people explained that they do this in their lives, but it felt funny once they brought attention to it.

Then they shook each other's hands while wanting the other person to see them or notice them, still without saying anything. Next, we shook hands, wanting people to respect us; then we shook each other's hands, wanting people to listen to us. This time, while shaking hands, I asked everyone to say to the other person, "I want you to listen to me," and next, "I want you to hear me." Both of these are subtly different. Everyone got into pairs and discussed what came up for them with each of the different handshakes. All of a sudden, the room erupted with conversation. The feedback from the whole class after this was profound and enlightening; each person's perspective was very different. Everybody seemed to experience reactions or feelings that arose depending on which belief story it related to, and everyone had reactions to wanting people to like, respect, or listen to them.

The next handshake we did was to want people to love us and to say, "I want you to love me," as they shook hands. I think this is a fundamental need, and it has become very normalized for many people to want someone to love them. But, I don't think this belief is true. It was interesting to watch how many smiles and laughter it brought in the room.

I explained that many people feel the feeling of emptiness in their heart, a longing to be loved. The feeling of an empty hole in their heart. I explained that I have observed many people trying to fill this hole with people or things of the world or addictions, and all they are trying to do is to take away the feeling of emptiness.

I believe this hole or emptiness in the heart cannot be filled by people, material possessions, or addictions. They are temporary fixes, and when you wake up in the morning, the hole is still there. So back to the process. Next, I got everyone to shake hands, this time saying out loud, "I don't need you to like me." They went around saying this to all the people in the class. Then they said, "I don't need you to see me," followed by, "I don't need you to respect me," "I don't need you to listen to me," and the last one, "I don't need you to love to me."

I was surprised by how hard it was for many people in the group to say, "I don't want you to love me." Some started crying, and others couldn't even say it. This brought my attention to just how strong the story is that people believe that someone in the world is meant to love them. We discussed this in small groups and another interesting discovery was that many men had trouble saying, "I don't need you to respect me."

Then we did another round of handshaking, this time saying, "I don't need you to like me; I like myself, and I am free." After, I had them say, "I don't need you to see me; I see myself, and I am free," "I don't need you to respect me; I respect myself, and I am free," "I don't need you to listen to me; I listen to myself, and I am free," and finally, "I don't need you to love to me; I love myself and I am free."

A look of joy and excitement appeared on everyone's faces as they shook each other's hands and took back their power. It was amazing, and as the class shared in their feedback, they felt a huge weight had been lifted off of them; they had a new sense of freedom. I wondered how many other people have the same belief that someone in the world is meant to love them, too?

I believe that many of our emotional experiences like stress, anxiety, depression and worry come from and lead back to "The Big Five," which are: wanting someone to love us, like us, see us, hear us and respect us. It can be a combination of a few of these beliefs, and in some cases, I've seen all of them.

Trust, abandonment, and fear issues all can stem from these untrue beliefs that someone outside of ourselves is meant to keep us happy.

Sometimes beliefs can be even subtler. I will use one of my belief stories, which was that people had betrayed me in my life. I have had many occasions where I felt people had betrayed me, from family members to friends to partners and my own children. But did they really betray me, or did they just betray the stories I have that, if you loved me, you wouldn't have done that, and if you love me, you wouldn't betray my trust? I was giving the power of how I felt to someone else. I realized that the betrayal story wasn't really the root story and that it stemmed back to the real story, which was the belief that someone was meant to love me. The feeling of betrayal was just a feeling covering up the deeper and larger underlying belief.

I sat in a café one day listening to two friends talking, both wanting the other one to hear them, both wanting the other one to like them, both wanting the other to respect them. I imagined what would happen if one of them didn't need to be heard, seen, or liked? And I saw that person just sitting, listening, and wondering, *how can I help this person to love and respect their self?*

Exercise 42.

Write your answers in your *Breaking Free* journal.

Title a new page: "The Big Five."

1. Do I want people to love me, and what would they need to do to show me they do?

2. Do I want people to like me, and what would they need to do to show me they do?

3. Do I want people to see me, and what would they need to do to show me they do?

4. Do I want people to listen to me, and what would they need to do to show me they do?

5. Do I want people to respect me, and what would they need to do to show me they do?

6. Why do you need other people to do things for you to make you feel happy? Why are you relying on others for your happiness?

Summary

Imagine what it would be like not to need anybody to love, like, see, listen, or respect you? How free would you feel not to need someone to do this for you? The only person that needs to love you unconditionally is yourself. When you love and accept yourself completely, there are no feelings of betrayal or abandonment.

I encourage you not to give the power of how you feel to anybody else. Take back your power, take back your heart, and take back your freedom.

Chapter 44

The Four Ways to Fill the God-Sized Hole in Your Heart

I believe we have this feeling of emptiness in our hearts, which seems to create a feeling of aloneness and separation from people and from the world. I have witnessed this occurrence in myself and seen it in others. I have observed people trying to fill this feeling of emptiness in many ways. Firstly, by wanting and getting other people to fill this emptiness for us. This seems to happen in many ways, some of which are: wanting people to love and care for us, wanting people to like us, wanting people to listen to what we have to say, wanting people to see and acknowledge us, wanting people to respect us, appreciate us, or accept us, wanting people for companionship, or simple things like wanting people to remember our birthdays or our names.

The second way to fill ourselves up is by using things of the world. Let's start with the obvious ones that take us away from feeling any emptiness, aloneness, or separation. They are in no particular order: drinking alcohol, taking social drugs, smoking cigarettes, eating food, having sex. I would call these addictions, but what are addictions? Why do we get addicted to something? I believe we get addicted to them because they fill up and take away the feeling of emptiness. They work, so we keep using them, but they are temporary and don't last, so we constantly need to go back to them for more. Coffee is a good example of this. You have a cup of coffee.

The drug caffeine affects your brain and central nervous system, blocking the effects of adenosine, which is a neurotransmitter that relaxes the brain and makes you feel tired. It speeds up your heart and circulates the blood around your body faster. All of these things make you feel more energy and more alive, but then the drug wears off. You start having withdrawal symptoms, and like most drugs, there is a downside, as the body has been over stimulated and the result is you feel more down and flat than you were to start off with, so you crave or need another coffee to pick you back up. Again, this is a common characteristic of many drugs and is a short-term fix.

The food I am referring to is the food that fills up the feeling of emptiness in our hearts, not food for nutrition. These foods have many appearances, and the supermarket shelves are packed with them. They range from highly sweetened foods, fast foods, biscuits, coffee, ice cream, chocolate, and all kinds of other "comfort foods." It's even funny that we call them that - comforting us from what? Is it our unhappiness, our lack of fulfillment, or is it what I believe is the emptiness in our hearts?

More examples of hole fillers are: shopping, overworking, sports, competition, gambling, pornography, socializing and entertainment, from music and movies to television and video games, Facebook and all of social media. There are many, many more. Some people may argue that these are just things we do to enjoy life, but my question is, what lies beneath them? What is driving us to seek out escapism and entertainment? We seem to be packing as much activity into our days as possible and never resting. We seem to have become more restless and relentless.

We don't even stop for lunch anymore, let alone have a morning or afternoon tea break. For some people, it seems they can't even go for a walk or a run without having headphones on. What is wrong with the silence? Or is it to drown out the overly busy minds, to block out the world? There could be many reasons, but even having a busy mind could be a way of keeping us from the quietness in stillness or loneliness. This is a clever strategy. We now have a back-up plan in case our minds become quiet while we are running or walking and the loneliness feeling appears: We can turn the music up! Of course, I'm not saying all people go running with headphones on because they don't like the quietness or that they get bored running. But this leads me to a point: Is the feeling of boredom just another impression of the emptiness?

Why do we seem to need to always be busy? I know this one for myself. I remember coming home for lunch to our family home when I was about 20 years old. When I got home, nobody was there, and I didn't like the quietness and being by myself so I would turn on the television to fill up the house with noise so I didn't have to feel the feeling of aloneness. I also do the keeping busy thing and used to constantly be looking for more projects, business ideas, and things to fix. I became aware of this, and I would watch myself doing it. Money fits into the list. We can spend an awful amount of time working to make money and think that somehow money will fill up the gap and make us feel fulfilled and happy. We know money can't buy us happiness, but it can buy us things, and we can be happy for a while. But then the novelty wears off, and emptiness comes back. Don't get me wrong; money is very useful. You can have great experiences and go to amazing places in the world. You can buy amazing handcrafted objects, and you can help people less fortunate than yourself. It can buy you houses, delicious food, holidays, and stuff. But after a while, your house is just a house, the stuff is just stuff, the food dissolves, and you are hungry again. The holidays are soon forgotten except for the thousands of photos you took to remember how happy you were. Then you have to come back to work, and the emptiness hole returns, except if you have a job that you love and look forward to everyday.

Food isn't a great way to fill up the emptiness. It digests out of your stomach, and you feel empty and hungry again. In fact, food has to be the worst one on the list for filling up the emptiness. You feel empty, you have a big meal, you feel full and content, and two hours later, you feel empty again. Damn! It's a very short-term fix, and you know what happens if you eat too much. Now you feel even emptier about the way you look, and it's a downward spiral from there. I have experienced this one myself. In truth, I have experienced most of these myself.

Our lives seem to be very full of people, things, and activities. A friend said to me that we have to do something in our lives, that we can't just do nothing, and I say it's not what you do; it's why you do it that's important. What is the true motivation for our actions or anything we do for that matter?

I believe most of us do the people things and the activity things and buying the material things just to fill up the empty hole in our hearts. We will do almost anything to avoid feeling empty and alone. We have this urging desire to be connected to someone or something, but when we wake up in the morning, the emptiness is back, so we need to start all over again to take away this feeling and fill the emptiness.

In my experience, none of these things really fill it up. I have spent my life trying them all, trying and finding what will work as a permanent solution. I have worked out that it's definitely not people. I have had all sorts of emotional hurts, pain, and disappointment chasing that one, and I have observed many people having emotional pain as they become obsessed about wanting people to love them and wanting them to fill their empty hearts. It's not drugs, alcohol, cigarettes, or coffee; it's not holidays, money, houses, or stuff. None seem to have a lasting affect.

I have discovered that humans can't fill the empty hole in your heart. It's not a money food or stuff-sized hole. I have come to realize it's a GOD-sized hole in your heart, and materials, things, and people cannot fill it up. It's not a religious God-sized hole, either; it's a connection-with-the-Oneness-sized hole, one that can only be filled by connecting to something greater than yourself and greater than each other. I believe when we come into this world, we have a kind of veil placed over us to stop us from having this clear and pure connection to something bigger than ourselves, and as human beings, we yearn and long for the reuniting and connection to the Oneness or the Dao or God, whatever you would like to call it. I'm not saying we are not always connected to it. I'm saying that many of us have lost the ability to see, hear, feel, and experience it. We have been convinced that life is something else.

I have experienced that there are four parts to get this connection back, and they are simple. Well, sort of simple.

Firstly, as I've mentioned, instead of wanting people to love you, like you, respect you, listen to you and see you, you can do this

247

for yourself: Stop seeking love and approval outside of yourself. Basically all you have to do is love, respect, and accept yourself unconditionally. But this also means you have to love and accept your dark side or shadow side as well, which are the parts you may not necessarily like about yourself or like about your character and your actions. How can you love anyone else unconditionally if you can't love yourself unconditionally? It's about not having an expectation that anybody is meant to love, like, see, listen, and respect you; this is for you to do for yourself. It's really that simple. Take back your power. Don't give the control and power of how you feel to someone else. You have the power.

Secondly, connect to the Oneness or Dao or God through nature. Spend time in nature every day - in the woods, forests, jungle, or native bush for New Zealanders. Spend time in the hills and mountains, by the streams and rivers. Spend time in and by the sea. Spend time with trees, plants, and flowers. Spend time in your garden. Be with birds and animals. All of these things will bring you back into connection with nature and the Oneness. Feel the rain. Watch the clouds. Observe the moon and stars. Feel the warmth of the sun on your skin. We all know how good we feel when we've had a day at the beach or when you have gone for a walk in nature or sat on a mountain looking at the beautiful view, or when you look up at the night sky with wonderment of the unknown. It's just that easy. And it's been under our noses all the time, a doorway into the Oneness, a true gift to all humankind. We live in it everyday, and we haven't necessarily seen it though it's right in front of us. It's a connection back to the Oneness for ourselves and for all human beings.

Thirdly is by practicing Qigong health exercises. It is well known that the Chinese have been studying and perfecting the art of moving energy or Qi inside the body for thousands of years. Traditional Chinese Medicine works with the dysfunction and imbalance of Qi in the body, so in saying this, practitioners of this art have perfected many ways of how to bring energy back into the heart if it is depleted. There are exercises in most Qigong exercise systems that tonify the heart Qi, not only from using the energy in the breath but by drawing energy into the body through acupuncture points. I believe this is why many of the old Chinese Qigong masters look like spring chickens; they look 50 years old when they are actually 90, and this is why I teach and practice Qigong daily myself - not necessarily to increase my longevity but because of the vitality and energy I get each day from the practice. If you haven't practiced Qigong before, try it and you will see what I mean.

And the Fourth way to fill the God-sized hole is simple: give your love away. Now that you love, like, see, hear, and respect yourself, and you don't need to get it from any other human being, give your love away. Give your love and kindness to others, to animals, birds, fish, plants, trees, rivers, the sea, and the planet. The secret is not to want anything back, but to give it away because you can. Remember there is nothing you can get from anybody or anything else that you can't give to yourself in a much purer form. When you give love and caring away to others, and you give love and self-acceptance to yourself, it's more powerful, stronger, cleaner, clearer, and purer, and in itself holds an ability, a doorway, to straight connection to the Oneness or God without any veils, deceptions, or distractions. It's simple, pure connection.

To fill the hole of longing and emptiness is as simple as that. And it will take practice. We generally don't live our lives like this. You also may have old patterns and underlying beliefs stories you may need to break. It's called a spiritual practice for a reason - because you need to practice loving yourself daily.

It's like seeing the world though new eyes without any veils and illusions. For you, it will be a changed world and a beautiful and loving way of living.

Practice these four ways, and it will transform you, your vision, your experience, and your life.

Be Free. Be Happy.

Much love and kindness,
Pete Caughey

BOOK CONCLUSION

I hope you have found the journey of my stories a useful springboard into your own belief stories, and that by reading and working through each chapter, it has been an interesting and insightful process for you. My wish for you is that you have some space around your opinions and beliefs and that you now question your points of view. I hope that you are more able to observe your reactions and the stakes you have placed in the ground, and then watch yourself defend them as truth.

The world has made up a way of existence to suit itself, but it does not benefit all of the earth's inhabitants who want to be free. Identifying our stories helps us to break free from the illusions of the world, which will also disempower our karmic imprint and ultimately lead us to become more conscious. This is the path to freedom.

You will have discovered that many of our stories link back to a few main core false beliefs such as thinking that someone in the world is meant to love you, like you, listen to you, see you, or respect you, and that these will fill up your heart and make you feel complete. Except, this is not true.

You will also now know how to fill the emptiness in your heart in positive ways so that you will always feel content, happy, and full without needing another person or physical thing to fill you up.

I hope this book has helped you make more sense out of your life and has shed light on your life's purpose.

Please share this book with the people you love and help them on their journey to be free as well.

Breathe in and expand your heart, then breathe out and expand your heart some more.

ABOUT PETER CAUGHEY

Peter is an Acupuncturist, a Doctor of Traditional Chinese Medicine (TCM) and a Master Qigong Practitioner. With his combined practice and teaching of TCM, Qigong and Taiji Quan he has over 25 years of experience.

Peter is an ex-Special Forces solider and spent 16 years in the New Zealand Military Armed Forces.

He is a Healer, a Warrior, a Husband, a Father, Writer, Philosopher, Teacher and an advocate of freedom for all.

He likes coaching people in managing and overcoming their stress and worry. He likes helping people to break free from limiting beliefs and stories about themselves and their relationships with others, that stop them from being free. He likes challenging peoples' points of view and introducing the possibility that there could be a different way to see themselves and see life itself.

Peter's passions aside from helping people are motorsports, rugby and he loves to travel the world with his wife Josephine and son Rayner, meeting new people and experiencing their cultures and their country.

To learn more, visit www.petercaughey.com and for Peter's online Qigong courses, visit www.forestrock.com

Made in the USA
Monee, IL
15 October 2020

45102477R00163